James Bignon
Timeless Gospel Music Collection

Songs written and arranged by James Bignon

JAMES BIGNON

AuthorHouse™
1663 Liberty Drive
Bloomington, IN 47403
www.authorhouse.com
Phone: 1-800-839-8640

Omni Global Network, Inc.
303 Perimeter Center North, Suite 300
Atlanta, Georgia 30346
Phone: 678.376.8000
Toll Free: 866.658.3336

Published by AuthorHouse 12/05/2012

ISBN: 978-1-4772-8394-3 (sc)
ISBN: 978-1-4772-8395-0 (e)

Library of Congress Control Number: 2012920110

This book is printed on acid-free paper.

Dedication

To my mother Eula M. Bignon

It is with the greatest honor and humility that I dedicate this songbook to my darling mother, Eula M. Bignon. As a child I had no idea that your passion for God and his music would become so interwoven in my life and is even now apparent in your grandchildren.

Every song I've penned in this book embodies priceless moments of you encouraging me to write lyrics that people can hold on to and feel the presence of God as they sing.

I love you and thank you for *"Everything You've Done for Me"*.

FOREWORD

I've dedicated my life to gospel music. As a child I saw the affect it had on the believer. It was astonishing to see so many people hanging on to every word in a good gospel song. To see the sincerity in their eyes, the raised or clasped hands, the facial expressions showing thanks, acceptance, encouragement and hope made an unforgettable impression on me. I heard people singing and playing the same songs over and over again with increased excitement every time. They All Inspired Me.

I wanted to write songs that would have that effect. I've been recording gospel music for several years now and have been quite fortunate to have acquired a catalogue of songs that have proven to be a blessing to so many. This songbook is a collection of a few of those songs. Let them give you inspiration. Let them help point you in the right direction. Let them help you rise above your circumstance. Let them help empower you to help someone else. Let them draw you closer to God.

James Bignon

CONTENTS

If I Hold Out 1
Who He Is 7
He Is God 13
For The Rest Of My Life 19
How Excellent Is Thy Name 25
God Is Great 30
My Offering 36
More Than I Can Say 42
He Made The Difference 48
I Can't Thank Him Enough 56
I'm Believing God For A Miracle 63
Just Because He Is Who He Is 73
Lead Sheet Only 78
Just For Me 79
This Is The Day 85
On The Other Side Of Through 91
I Came To Lift Him Up 97
Lord, I Thank You 103
I'm Gonna Do Your Will 109
Praise The Matchless Lamb Of God 115
What A Time 121
Magnify The Lord 127
None Like Him 133
Heaven Belongs To You 139

If I Hold Out

(My Change Will Come)

Bridge I
my change will come Trou - - ble don't last
al - ways Trou - ble don't last al - ways Thank God
it don't last al - - ways I can feel
my bless - ing com - ing on
1.
Repeat from M4

20
2, 3.
G min
G
F
F
G min
E
F
E♭
B♭
D
Verse
There's no need to wor - ry
23
F
A
B♭
no need to des - pair
Je - sus knows
26
F
A
B♭
C min
A
he knows my eve - ry care
29
F♯-5
D
D 7sus4
G
I'm walk - ing by faith
my faith

31
B aug
C m7/C
Unison:Choir
— is what I'm hold - - - ing to I know
33
D m7/D
E♭m7/E♭
he will see — me through He —
35
2d x: Go to VAMP M37
A♭
G min
A♭
Go to Chorus M4 then, Verse & Vamp
S/A/T
Lead
— knows just What to do If I hold
37
Lead: Ad-Lib (Consult CD)
39
A♭/B♭
G min/B♭
A♭/B♭
VAMP
S/A/T
to do
If I

40
wait
my change will come
43
2nd x: Go to M-47
If I wait
my
46
4.
Repeat from M39
47
Bridge II
change will come
change will come
Trou
48
ble don't last
al - ways
Trou - ble don't last

51
al - - - ways Thank God it don't last
53
2d x: To End go to M56
al - ways I can feel my bless - ing com - ing on
55
5.
Repeat from M48
56
Trou
F9sus4
If I
58
Fine
wait
my change will come

Who He Is

Scored by
James Bignon
=90
Writer / Arranger
James Bignon
Lead & S/A/T
Intro:
Piano
Ab2d/Ab
Db/Ab
Verse
V1. Big e - nough
Eb/Ab
Db/Ab
to be eve - ry - where
Ab
Db/Ab
Per-son-al e - nough that
Eb/Ab
Db/Ab
Edim/C
when I need him he's there
Fmin/F
Cmin7
Awe-some God

10
E♭sus4/G♭
A♭sus4/E♭
11
12
that he is
He loves me
13
A♭
D♭/A♭
14 E♭/A♭
D♭/A♭
15 A♭
D♭/A♭
Verse II
Hea-ven and earth pro-claim his ma - jes-ty
his han-dy work is
16
E♭/A♭
D♭/A♭
D♭
Edim
B♭
Fmin/C
17
E♭/C
E♭
18
A♭9sus4/G♭
E♭7sus4
writ-ten in lifes ta-pes - try
Awe-some God that he is
He
19
A♭
D♭/A♭
E♭
20 E♭/A♭
Fmin
E♭
Fmin
E♭
21 D♭
Chorus (SAT))
loves me
And I give him praise for Who He Is

Fmin
A♭6/D♭
E♭
Cmin7
my life ce - le - brates Who He Is
let eve - ry voice be
A♭6/D♭
Fmin
B♭min7/G♭
A♭sus4/E♭
raised for Who He Is
He's the match - less lamb of God
That's Who He Is
Fsus4/D♭
A♭
D♭/A♭
E♭/A♭
D♭/A♭
A♭/C
Verse III
It's a-ma - zing all he does for me
I'm so un - wor - thy

E♭/A♭ D♭/A♭ Cmin7 E♭sus4/G♭ A♭sus4/E♭
still he keeps on bless - ing me Awe-some God that he is He
A♭ Fmin E♭ Fmin/C E♭ D♭
Chorus II
loves me And I give him praise for Who He Is
B♭sus4/C A♭/E♭
My life ce - le - brates Who He Is let eve - ry voice be
Cm11/D♭ E♭ Fmin B♭min7/G♭ A♭sus4/E♭
raised for Who He Is He's the match - less lamb of God

Chorus III
Yes! I give him praise for Who He Is my life ce-le-
brates Who He Is let eve-ry voice be raised for Who He Is
He's the match-less lamb of God He's the
match-less lamb of God That's Who He Is

57
58
That's Who He Is
59
60
61
That's Who He Is
62
63
That's Who He Is
64
65
66
Fine
Lead
That's Who He Is

He Is God

Scored by
James Bignon
♩ = 100
Writers / Arrangers
James Bignon III & Christopher Bignon
Music Arrangement
M.D. Stokes
Piano
Intro
E♭min
D♭
E♭min
D♭
E♭min/B♭
D dim
E♭sus
E♭7/G
B Maj7
D♭
D♭7/B
E♭min7
E♭m7(♯5)/A♭
D♭
D♭
E♭min7
Ld & S/A/T
E♭sus4/B♭
CHORUS
11
King of Kings
and Lord of Lords

12
cre - a - tor of all
He is my fa -
14
E♭min7/B♭
B♭7/D
E♭sus4
E♭/G
A♭m9/B
- - ther do you know he is
Al - pha and O - me -
To: Ending 3, V2 (M28), Pg4
To: Ending 4, Bridge (M-37), pg5
To: Ending 5, Go to (M-55), Pg6
To VAMP: Ending 6, Go to (M-56), Pg6
16
E♭min7/B
E♭min/A♭
- - ga be - gin - ing and end
He is my eve -
D♭
E♭min7
18
E♭min/B♭
B♭7/D
Repeat 1x
1.
2.
ry - thing King of Kings
ry - thing He is God

20
Verse I
Fm7(♯5)
< Italic: 2d Lead >
B♭sus7♯5
Let me tell you about a man I know He's the shep-herd and the bis-hop of my soul, No
I know
22
Fm7(♯5)
B♭sus7♯5
games No tricks He is the Great I Am
No jokes No scams He is the
24
E♭9sus4
E♭min7/B
Duet
way the truth and the light when I'm struggl-ing through hard times
26
A♭min7
E♭m7/G♭
Duet
Fm7(♭5)
B♭aug
Go to Chorus (M-11)
He told me to keep my head up high for he's al-ways on time
S/A/T
King of Kings

28
E♭min/B♭ B♭7/D
3.
E♭m
Verse II < Italic: 2d Lead >
Duet
ry - thing He is God Who do you know could save a wretch like me a
30
Duet
Duet
sin - ner like me? He saved and set free picked me up turned me a-round and he placed my feet
32
on so-lid ground But who am I that he is mind - ful of me
OO - O-O-O-Oooo
34
EM9
A♭min7
B♭m7♯5/G♭
calls me friend I'm glad he's think-ing of me my Mas-ter my Fat-her
my Sav-iour my Friend

36
Fm7(♭5) B♭aug
Go To Chorus (M-11)
37
to Bridge...
E♭min/B♭
B♭7/D
he is the Great I Am
He is my eve - ry - thing
E♭min/A♭
King of Kings
39
Bridge
Choir
E♭m
B♭min7
E♭/G
A♭min
E♭min7/C
D♭
King of Glo - ry O! so ho - ly
43
B♭min7
match - less lamb of God
D♭/E♭
E♭/G
G dim
F dim
B♭dim
A♭min
B9
B♭7
47
E♭min
B♭min7
E♭
E♭
F dim
G dim
A♭min
A♭min
Rose of Sha - ron Light of

50
hea - ven match - less lamb of God
Go To Chorus (M-11)
55
Repeat Chorus (M-11) 1x
56
VAMP
54
5.
6.
King of Kings ry-thing King of Kings ry-thing He is God
57
Lead Ad-Libs
To End: Go to M-61
60
Repeating M's 57-60 is Optional
61
Lead: Occapella
Fine
He is God He is God He is God

FOR THE REST OF MY LIFE

Writer / Arranger
James Bignon

Scored by
James Bignon

14
E♭
Gmin7
A♭Maj7
want you to do what - e - ver you want to
17
Cmin
Cmin/A
B♭/A♭
do
Lord, this ve - ry day
20
E♭/G
Fmin/A♭
E♭/G
Fmin
E♭
EmM7♭5/D♭
D♭m(maj7)/C
Cm7(♯5)/F
Choir
Yes! this ve - ry hour I'm yours Yours
23
E♭(add2)/G
E♭/A♭
E♭m6♭5
Cm7♯5/B♭
Lead
Cmin/E♭
B♭/D
Choir
For the rest
I've made up my mind yours For the

Chorus I
(Leader Ad-Lib)
26
Cmin A♭Maj7 Gmin7 E♭ E♭/A♭ Cm7(♯5)/B♭ G7
rest of my life I'll serve you For the
30
Cmin/E♭ Gmin7 E♭ A♭/B♭ E♭/A♭ A♭ B♭/G Cmin/E♭ B♭/D
rest of my days have your way For the
34
Cmin B♭/G E♭/F E♭
rest of my life I'll do your bless - ed will
38
Gmin7 E♭/A♭ E♭/G A♭/B♭
Lord I'll do your bless - ed will

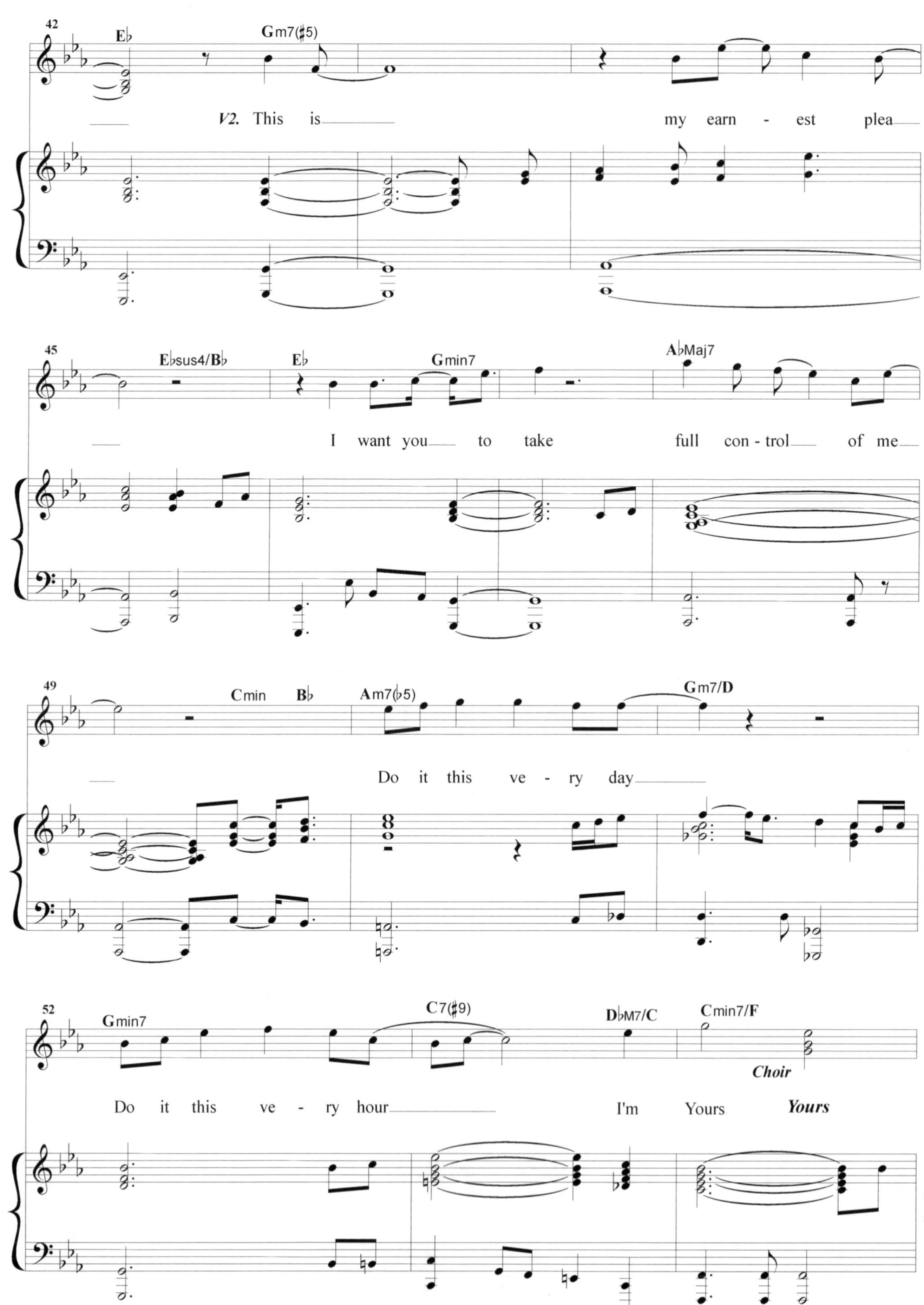
42
E♭
Gm7(♯5)
V2. This is
my earn - est plea
45
E♭sus4/B♭
E♭
Gmin7
A♭Maj7
I want you to take full con - trol of me
49
Cmin
B♭
Am7(♭5)
Gm7/D
Do it this ve - ry day
52
Gmin7
C7(♯9)
D♭M7/C
Cmin7/F
Choir
Do it this ve - ry hour
I'm Yours
Yours

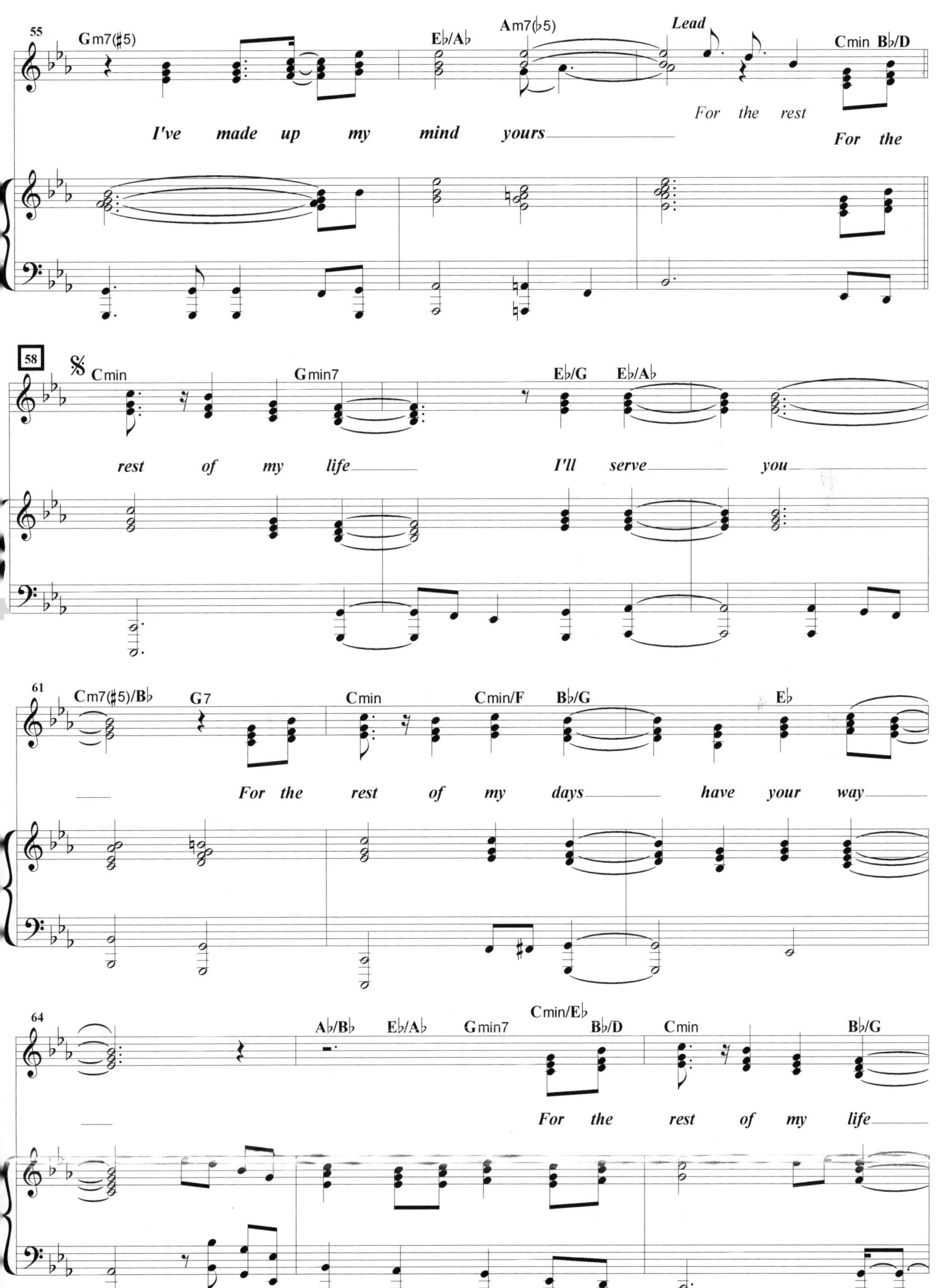
55
Gm7(♯5)
E♭/A♭
Am7(♭5)
Lead
Cmin B♭/D
For the rest
I've made up my mind yours
For the
58
Cmin
Gmin7
E♭/G E♭/A♭
rest of my life
I'll serve you
61
Cm7(♯5)/B♭
G7
Cmin
Cmin/F
B♭/G
E♭
For the rest of my days have your way
64
A♭/B♭
E♭/A♭
Gmin7
Cmin/E♭
B♭/D
Cmin
B♭/G
For the rest of my life

67
To End, Go to Vamp (M-76)
I'll do your bless - ed will
71
Lord I'll do your bless - ed will
74
Repeat Chorus from M-58 as desired
76
Vamp
For the Lord I'll do
77
1
Repeat 2 times or as desired
2
Fine
your bless - ed will

How Excellent Is Thy Name

7
Repeat 1 time
How ex - cel - lent is thy name
9
Unison: S/A
2d Time - Go to M-12
How ex - cel - lent is thy name
11
2
Repeat Chorus from M-6
12
To Verse
How

13
VERSE
When I look a - round and see
15
eve - ry - thing you've done for me
17
I have to give you the praise

19
Chorus
Choir
give you the praise for the vic - to - ry How
21
Repeat 1 time
ex - cel - lent is
How
23
Unison: S/A
ex - cel - lent is thy name
How

25
Choir
ex - cel - lent is thy name
How
27
Repeat 1 time
ex - cel - lent is
How
29
Unison: S/A
ex - cel - lent is thy name
How
31
Fine
Choir
ex - cel - lent is thy name

GOD IS GREAT

Scored by
James Bignon

Writer / Arranger
James Bignon

10
B♭ A♭/B♭ A♭/B♭ E♭/B♭ B♭/A♭ A/F B♭
God is great and great - ly to be praised God is great and
13
great - ly to be praised God is great and
15
B♭/D F E/F F
great - ly to be praised If he does - n't do
17
S/A: Unison S/A/T
D E G♭ G Caug7/D E♭7
any - thing - else He's al - rea - dy done

19
S/A: Unison
Ab
Eb/F
Bb
Bbmin
Eb7
Caug7/D
After Verse 1, Go to M-37 (V2)
more than e - nough He's al - rea - dy done
Repeat from Chorus M-8
21
1. Ab
Eb/G
Bb/D
2.
Bb/D
more than e - nough
more than e - nough
23
Eb
Eb/F
Bb/D
Eb
Bb/F
Ab2d
Lead
1. When I look back o - ver my life I can
26
clear - ly see that the Lord has sur - ly

29
E♭
B♭/E
E♭/F
B♭
F
S/A/T
been good to me
And if he does-
31
D
Edim
G♭dim
Gmin
S/A: Unison
n't do
any - thing - else
He's al -
33
B♭/D
E♭
A♭
E♭/F
B♭
B♭min
S/A/T
S/A: Unison
rea - dy done
more than e - nough
He's al -
35
E♭/F
B♭
B♭min
3. Go to Chorus M-8, then to M-37 (V2)
37
B♭/D
S/A/T
rea-dy done
more than e-nough
more than enough

38
E♭ E♭/F B♭/D E♭ B♭/F A♭2d
Lead
2. From sink - ing sand He
41
B♭/D E♭ E♭/F B♭/D
lift - ed me My soul is re - joic - ing
44
E♭ B♭/E E♭/F B♭ F
S/A/T
Be - cause he set me free And if he does -
46
D Edim G♭dim Gmin
S/A: Unison
n't do any - thing - else He's al -

48
B♭/D
E♭
A♭
E♭/G
S/A/T
rea - dy done
more than e - nough
S/A: Unison
He's al -
50
S/A/T
rea - dy done
more than e - nough
S/A: Unison
He's al -
52
S/A/T
rea - dy done
more than e - nough
S/A: Unison
He's al -
54
S/A/T
rea - dy done
more than e - nough
Fine

MY OFFERING

Scored by
James Bignon
= 100
Writer / Arranger
James Bignon
Lead
Intro:
S/A/T
Piano
VERSE
V1. Lord you've gi - ven me more than words could e - ver say

13
and when I count my bless - ings the ma - ny times
16
you've made a way
18
I can't help but thank you for eve - ry - thing you've done so
22
please ac - cept my of - fer - ing to you God's on - ly

VERSE II
Lead II
son I know I don't de - serve I don't de - serve all
of this good Lord, you've tru - ly blessed me and I'm trying to
do all that I should
{ Duet }
I can't help but thank
you
Lead I
for eve - ry - thing you've done so

37
{ Duet }
Lead I
please ac - cept my of - fer - ing to you God's on - ly son
40
CHORUS I
*** Leader: Ad-Lib after each choir line ***
I give you my heart I give you my
43
mind I give you my soul
46
Please take con - trol Just as I

49
am
Lord Je - sus I come
Here I am Lord Here I am Lord
52
This is my of - fer - ing to you God's on - ly son
55
CHORUS II
Leader: Ad-Lib before each choir line
I give you my heart
58
I give you my mind
I give you my

61
soul
Please
take con - trol
Just as I
65
{ Duet }
am
Lord Je - sus I come
This is my of -
Here I am Lord Here I am Lord
69
Repeat from M-69, 1x or as desired
fer-ing to you God's on - ly son
This is my of -
73
Fine
fer-ing to you God's on - ly son

MORE THAN I CAN SAY

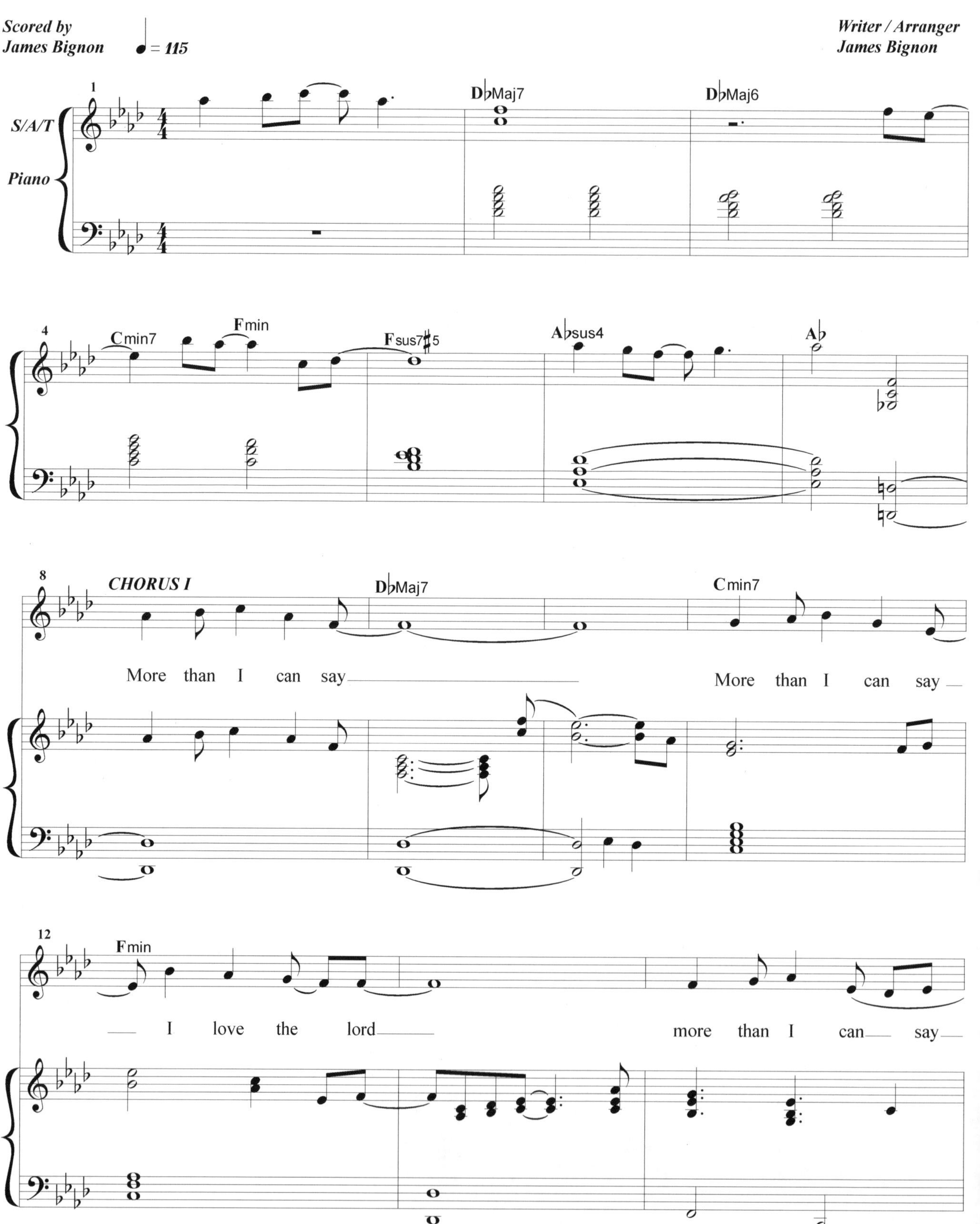

15
B♭min7
Cmin7
D♭Maj7
E♭
A♭
S/A/T
E♭/B♭
A♭/C
B♭min
A♭
A♭
D♭
He's the lov - er of my soul
19
S/A: Unison
E♭
D♭
Cmin7
Fmin
E♭/F
E♭
I praise him eve - ry - day
I love him much
22
D♭2d/E♭
DM7(♭5)/E♭
more than I can say
25
CHORUS II
26
More than I can say

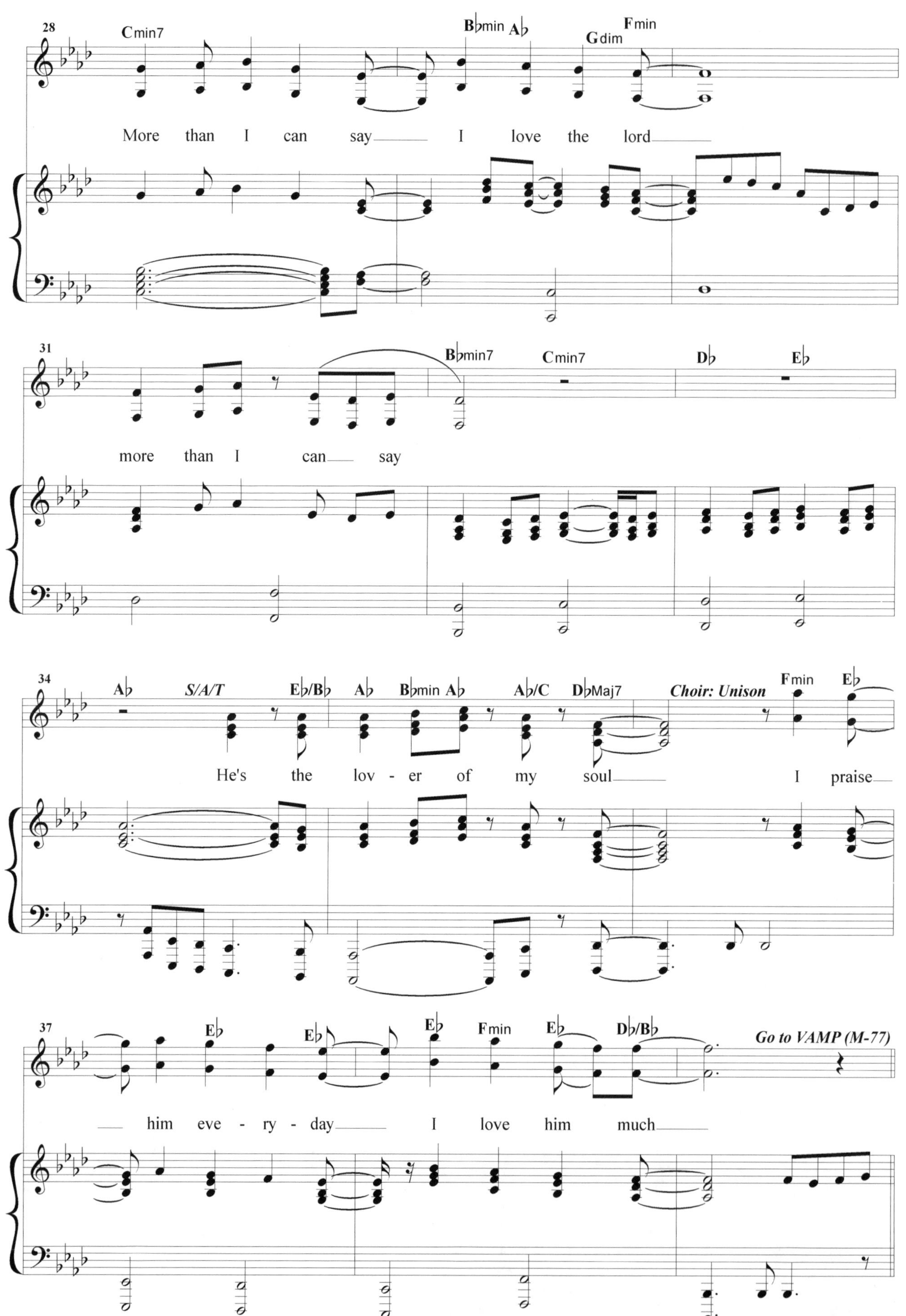
28
Cmin7
B♭min A♭
Gdim
Fmin
More than I can say I love the lord
31
B♭min7
Cmin7
D♭
E♭
more than I can say
34
A♭
S/A/T
E♭/B♭
A♭
B♭min A♭
A♭/C
D♭Maj7
Choir: Unison
Fmin
E♭
He's the lov - er of my soul I praise
37
E♭
E♭
E♭
Fmin
E♭
D♭/B♭
Go to VAMP (M-77)
him eve - ry - day I love him much

40
D♭/E♭
After V1, Go to V2 (M-59)
A♭
A♭sus4/E♭
more than I can say
VERSE
43
E♭sus4/A♭
Cm7
D♭Maj7
V1. Be-cause of Christ I'm brand new
47
A♭
E♭/C
A♭
A♭/D♭
D♭
E♭
Be-cause of him Life is worth liv - ing
51
A♭
E♭/C
A♭B♭min
A♭
Fmin
E♭/F
He's eve-ry-thing I need - ed I love him much

55
D♭/B♭
A♭
A♭sus4/E♭
more than I can say
58
Go to Chorus M-26 then, to M-59 (V2)
59
< To Verse II >
More than I can say
Csus♭5/D
A♭
A♭sus4
61
VERSE
A♭(omit5)
E♭/C
A♭/D♭
V2. I would be noth - ing with - out him
65
A♭
He makes my life so com - plete

69
A♭
E♭/C
D♭Maj7
A♭/D♭
E♭/F
E♭/C
I can best ex - plain this way
I love him much
73
D♭/B♭
Go to Chorus (M-26)
more than I can say
More than I can say
77
VAMP
D♭/E♭
A♭
A♭
E♭/C
Fmin
E♭
B♭min
Repeat 1 time
Choir: Unison
More than I can say
I love him much
81
D♭/E♭
A♭
D♭/F
E♭
A♭
Fine
More than I can say

HE MADE THE DIFFERENCE

Scored by
James Bignon ♩= 90

Writer / Arranger
James Bignon

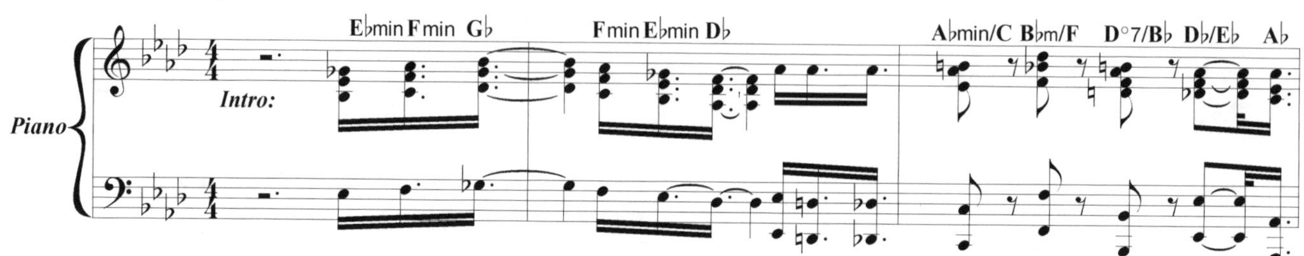

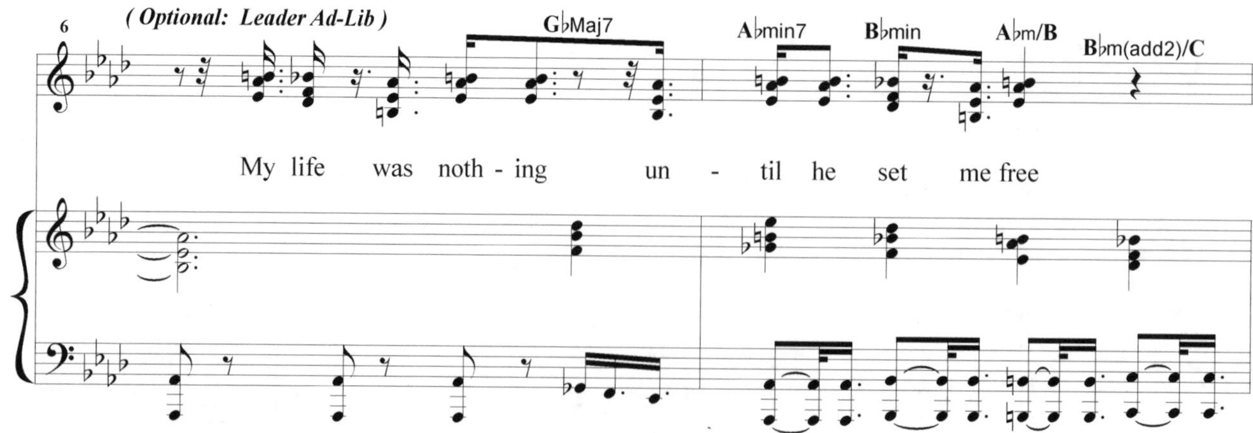

8
D♭7
What a change he made in my life
D♭7
Caug7
A♭m♭9/B
B♭7
10
A♭7
D♭/F
no more com - pro - mis - ing the wrong for the right
A♭7
A♭min/E♭
G♭
Choir
He made
Repeat Verse 1 time then, Go to Chorus
12
G♭Maj7/F
D♭
Unison: S/A
the dif-fe-rence He made the dif - ference in my life
A♭min/C
B♭min/F
B♭7(♭9)
Fm7(♯5)/E♭
A♭

14
CHORUS
I don't walk like I use to walk
I don't live like I use to live
D♭/F
15
He made the dif - fe - rence
Bdim/F
16
After Verse 2, Go to Bridge (M-31)
I don't talk like I use to talk
I don't give like I use to give

Repeat 1 time from M-14, Line 2
17
1.
He made the dif - fe - rence
A♭7
18
2.
A♭min/E♭
B♭m7(♯5)/G♭
He made the dif - fe - rence He made
19
A♭min/C
B♭min/F
B♭7(♭9)
Fm7(♯5)/E♭
A♭7
Unison: S/A
Choir
the dif - fe-rence He made the dif - ference in my life

21
A♭min
V2. He gives me joy that can-not be sur - passed
23
G♭Maj7
A♭min7
B♭min
A♭m/B
B♭m(add2)/C
I'm on a cloud from the first mo-ment to the last He
25
D♭7
D♭7
Caug7
A♭m♭9/B
B♭7
A♭7
walks with me talks with me tell-ing me I'm his own He

27
D♭/F
A♭7
A♭min/E♭
B♭m7(♯5)/G♭
calms all my fears telling me I am not a - lone
Choir
He made
29
G♭Maj7/F
Go to Chorus (M-14) then, To Bridge
A♭min/C
B♭min/F
B♭7(♭9)
Fm7(♯5)/E♭
A♭7
Unison: S/A
the dif - fe - rence He made the dif - ference in my life
31
Lead
What a change
He made the dif - fe - rence

32
(Leader Ad-Lib)
What a change
Choir
What a change
34
Go to Vamp (M-36)
3.
Repeat as desired then, Go to Vamp
What a change
What a change
What a change
36
4.
VAMP
(Lead)
I'm glad a - bout it
What a change
Choir I'm glad a - bout it

38
Leader: Ad-Libs
Choir
I'm glad a - bout it
Choir
I'm glad a - bout it
40
5.
Repeat as desired
(Lead)
I'm glad a
I'm glad a - bout it
41
B/E♭
G♭
Choir
I'm glad a - bout it He made
42
the dif - fer - ence
Unison: S/A
He made the
B/C
B♭min/F
B/B♭
D♭M/E♭
A♭
Fine
Choir
dif - ference in my life

I Can't Thank Him Enough

18
I'm so great - ful
I can't com - plain
He's been a good friend
faith - ful and true
22
He has kept me
through the storm and the
He has done
- Eve - ry - thing he said he would
26
CHORUS
rain
(Choir)
I can't thank him enough
Lead
I can't
do
30
thank him
I can't thank him e-nough
I can't

34
thank him e - nough
I can't
thank him e - nough
He's been
38
good
Good
So Good
So Good
42
I can't
I can't
thank him e - nough
Can't
46
thank him
I can't
thank him e - nough
I can't

50
thank him
I can't
thank him e-nough
I can't
54
thank him e-nough
For eve-ry-thing
(Choir)
For
58
eve-ry-thing he's
Go to M-58, then to Ending 2
62
1.
done
For eve-ry-thing
for

66
2.
done
For eve - ry - thing
for
70
a. After V2, Go to M-78 & VAM
eve - ry - thing
he's
74
Go To Verse 2, M-10
done
78
3.
done
I can't

81
VAMP
To End, Go to M-54
thank him e-nough
I can't thank him e-nough
I can't
85
Repeat VAMP as desired
thank him
I can't thank him e-nough
I can't
89
done
I can't thank him e-nough
I can't
96
thank him
e - nough
Fine

103

I'm Believing God For A Miracle

Scored by
James Bignon

Writer / Arranger
James Bignon

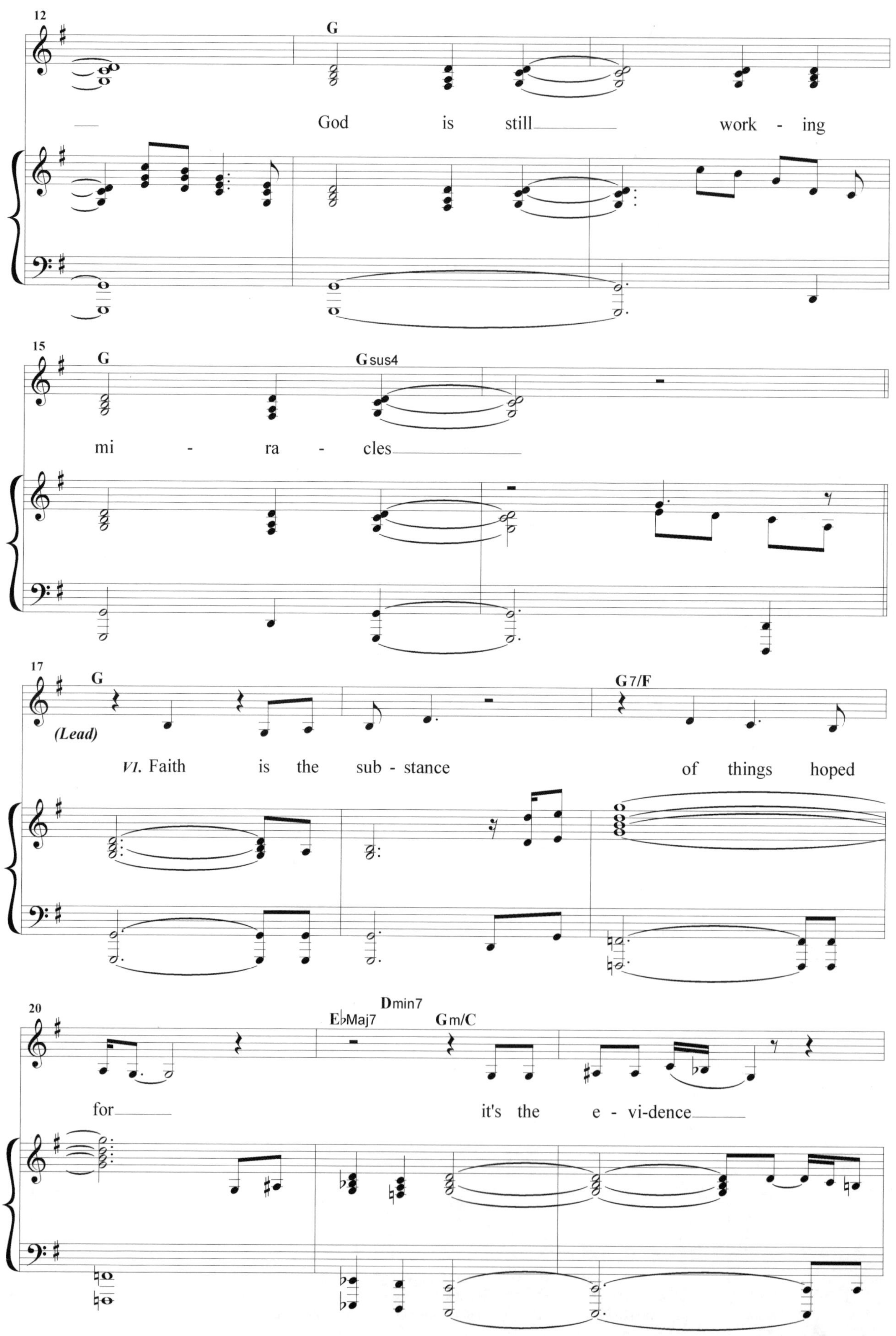
12
G
God is still working
15
G
Gsus4
mi - ra - cles
17
G
G7/F
(Lead)
V1. Faith is the sub - stance of things hoped
20
E♭Maj7
Dmin7
Gm/C
for it's the e - vi-dence

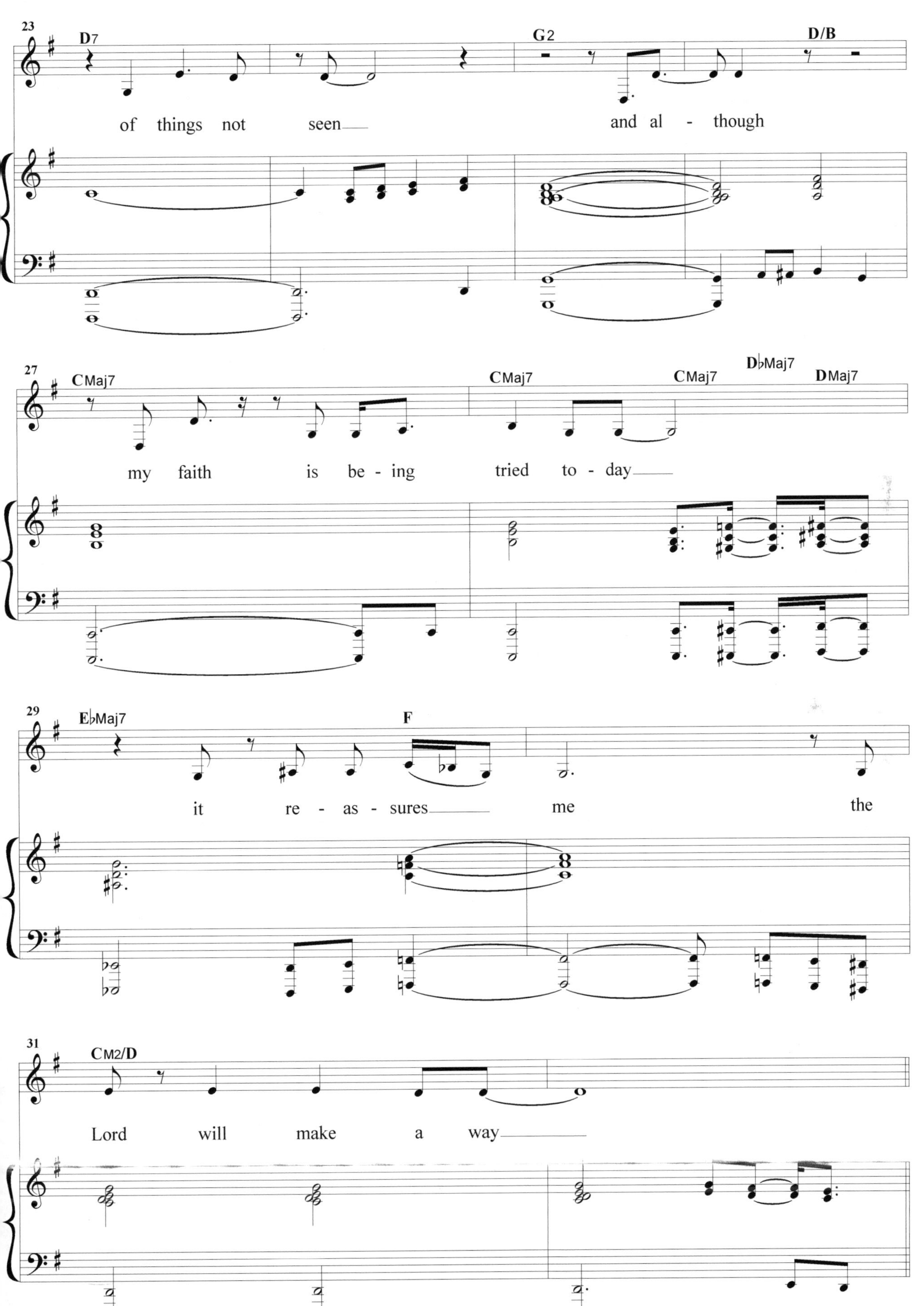
23
D7
G2
D/B
of things not seen
and al - though
27
CMaj7
CMaj7
CMaj7
D♭Maj7
DMaj7
my faith is be - ing tried to - day
29
E♭Maj7
F
it re - as - sures me the
31
CM2/D
Lord will make a way

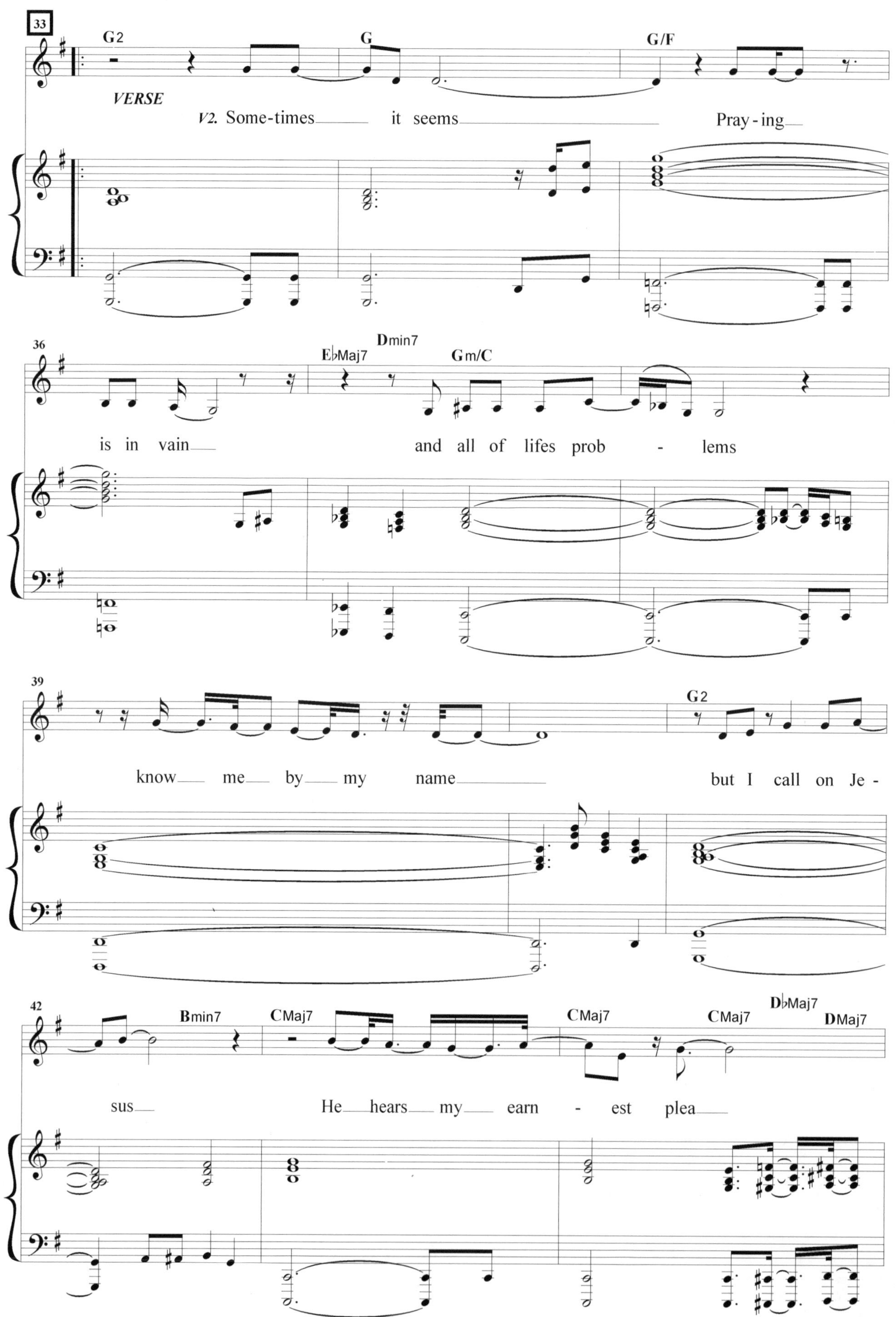
33
G2
G
G/F
VERSE
V2. Some-times it seems Pray-ing
36
E♭Maj7
Dmin7
Gm/C
is in vain and all of lifes prob - lems
39
G2
know me by my name but I call on Je -
42
Bmin7
CMaj7
CMaj7
CMaj7
D♭Maj7
DMaj7
sus He hears my earn - est plea

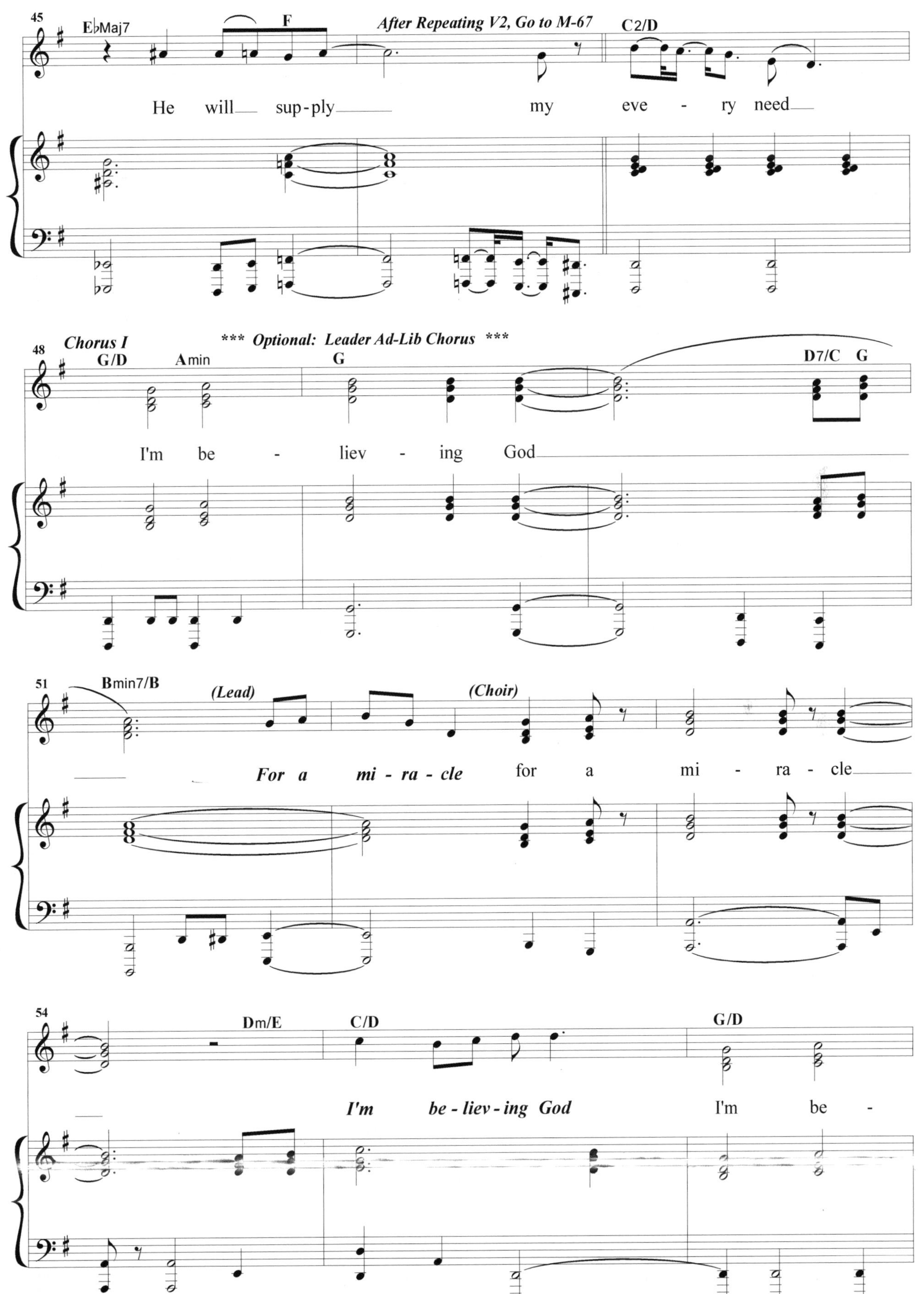
45
E♭Maj7
F
After Repeating V2, Go to M-67
C2/D
He will sup-ply my eve - ry need
48
Chorus I
*** Optional: Leader Ad-Lib Chorus ***
G/D
Amin
G
D7/C
G
I'm be - liev - ing God
51
Bmin7/B
(Lead)
(Choir)
For a mi - ra - cle
for a mi - ra - cle
54
Dm/E
C/D
G/D
I'm be - liev - ing God
I'm be -

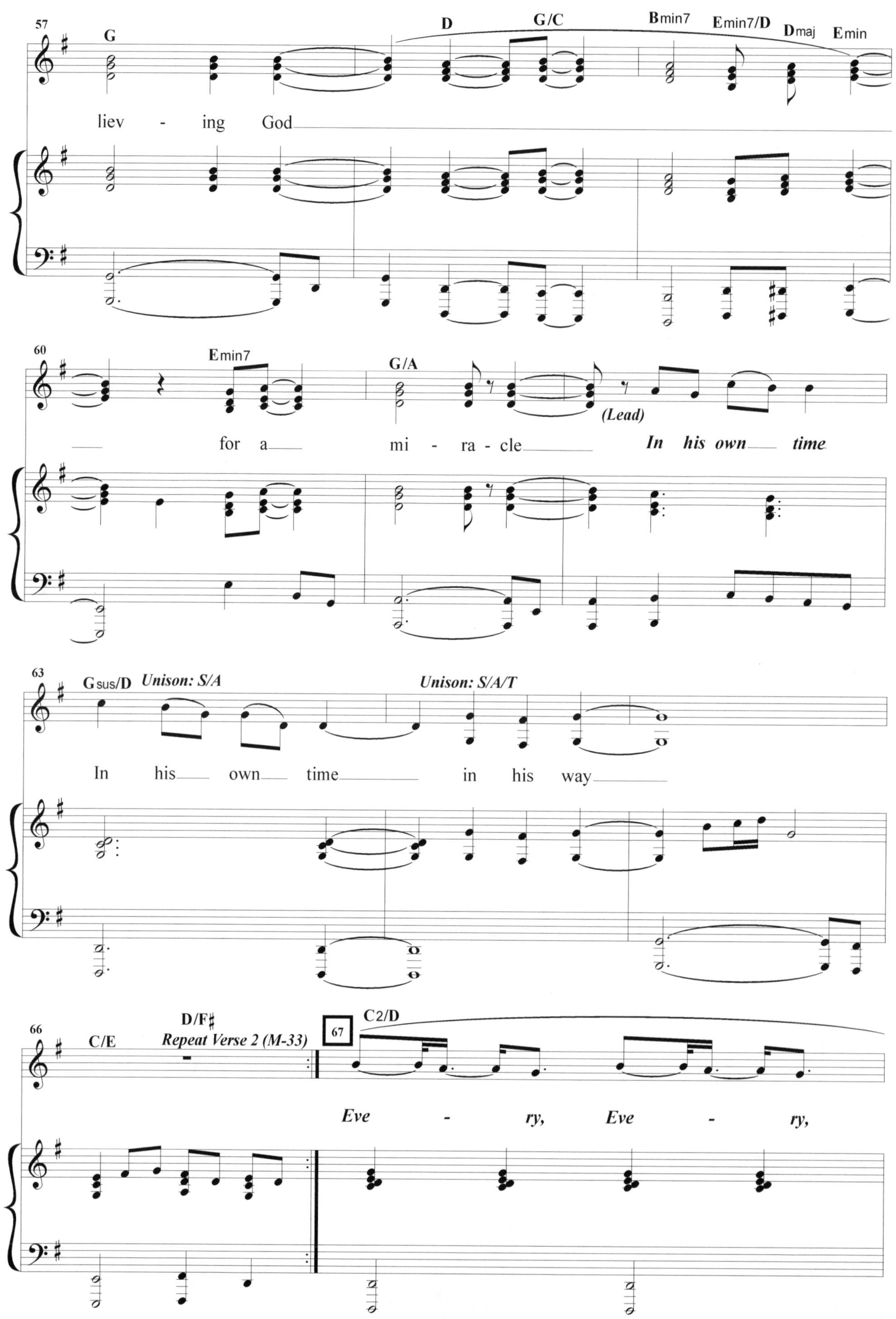
57
G
D
G/C
Bmin7
Emin7/D
Dmaj
Emin
liev - ing God
60
Emin7
G/A
for a mi - ra - cle
(Lead)
In his own time
63
Gsus/D
Unison: S/A
Unison: S/A/T
In his own time in his way
66
C/E
D/F♯
Repeat Verse 2 (M-33)
67
C2/D
Eve - ry, Eve - ry,

68
C2/D
B2/D♭
C2/D
D♭2/E♭
Eve - ry
My
eve - ry need
CHORUS II
70
A♭/E♭
B♭m/E♭
A♭
E♭/DA♭
I'm be - liev - ing God
74
A♭/C
B♭min7/A♭
A♭/B♭
E♭/F
D♭/E♭
for a mi - ra - cle
78
A♭
E♭
I'm be - liev - ing God

81
Cmin7
Fmin
Fmin7
(Choir)
for a
Ab/Bb
mi - ra - cle
84
Fm7(#5)/Eb
Unison: S/A/T
Unison: S/A
In his own time
In his way
BRIDGE
87
Bbm7#5/Ab
Ab/C
(Lead)
I don't know how
89
Ab/Db
(Choir)
I don't know how he's going to do it

92
(Lead)
(Choir)
Cmin7
Cmin/G
I don't know
I don't know when it will be done
95
E♭min7
A♭
D♭Maj7
by faith I
98
D♭Maj7
know I'll be de - li - vered
A♭/D♭
B♭min/F A♭
101
B♭min
A♭/C
Fmin7
A♭sus/E♭
Unison: S/A/T
Unison: S/A
In his own time
In his way

103
G♭/D♭
B♭min/F
Repeat Chorus (M-89) as desired
105
2.
(Lead)
In his own time
107
Repeat as desired
Unison: S/A
In his own time In his way
109
D♭/F
E♭/G
A♭
Fine

Just Because He Is Who He Is

Scored by
James Bignon ♩ = 145

Writer / Arranger
James Bignon

16
Db
Db/F
Gb
Db/Ab
Gb/Bb
Db
Db7/B
Db7/B
BMaj7
Ebmin7/Db
Db7/B
Db7/B
(Lead) Who he is
(Lead)
Choir
He is who he is
Glo - ry
Glo - ry
20
Gb/Bb
GbMaj7/F
Eb
Fmin
Gdim
Ab
Dbmin/Eb
(Lead)
Choir
(Lead)
Ho - nor
Ho - nor
Ma - jes - ty
23
Ab
Db
a. Repeat as desired then to Verses or
Choir
Ma - jes - ty be - longs to him
Db/Ab
C7/Bb
Cm7(b5)
26
FminGdim
VI. You can search the world o - ver

30
A♭
B♭min7/A♭
A♭
B♭min
A♭/C
D♭
D♭/F
G♭
D♭/A♭
G♭/B♭
D♭
you will find there's none like him
34
D♭7/B
BMaj7
D♭7/B
E♭min7/D♭
D♭7/B
G♭/B♭
G♭Maj7/F
E♭
Fmin
Gdim
All pow - er is in his hand
38
A♭
D♭min/E♭
A♭
D♭
Go to Chorus
He can de - stroy and he will de - fend
D♭/A♭
C7/B♭
Cm7(♭5)
42
(Lead)
Praise him
Choir
Praise him
(Lead)
Praise the lord
Choir
Praise the lord

46
Dbmin/F Ebm/Gb
Dbm/Ab B C
1. Repeat from M-42 as desired
(Lead) Praise him
Choir Praise him
(Lead) Praise the lord
Praise the lord
50
2. Dbm/Ab B C
51
B/F Gb
Dbmin/Ab
B/F Gb
(Lead) For who he is
(Lead) For who he is
Choir Praise the lord
For who he is
Choir For
54
Dbmin/Ab
3. Repeat from M-51 as desired
4. Dbmin/Ab
56
B/F Gb Dbmin/Ab
For
(Lead) King of Kings
That's
Choir who he is,
who he is
Choir King of Kings
58
B/F Gb Dbmin/Ab
B/F Gb Dbmin/Ab
who he is,
(Lead) Lord of Lords
That's
Choir That's who he is
Choir Lord of lords

62
B/F
G♭
D♭min/A♭
Repeat from M-56 as desired
who he is
(Lead) El Shad - dai
Choir That's who he is
65
D♭min/A♭
B/F
G♭
(Lead) That's who
(Lead) Je -
Choir El Shad - dai
That's who he is
68
B/F
G♭
D♭min/A♭
ho - vah Ra - pha
That's who
Choir Je ho - vah Ra - pha
Choir That's
71
D♭min/A♭
Repeat from M-64 as desired
B
G♭/B♭
D♭min
Fine
(Lead) Eve - ry-bo - dy
who he is
Praise Him

LEAD SHEET ONLY

Just For Me

Scored by
James Bignon ♩= 115

Writer / Arranger
James Bignon

18
A♭Maj7
Gsus4/D
Gaug7
Cmin
Go to Verse 2 (M-60)
Thank you
Thank you
Lord
23
1.
Repeat 1 time
2.
Cmin
C7(♯5)/G♭
27
E♭6(♭5)/F
VERSE
Lead
G♭6(♭5)/D
Gaug7
For eve - ry strip you let them place on your back I say
31
Cmin
Dm7(♯5)/C
B♭
Thank You
Choir
Thank you Lord
Thank you Lord

35
B♭7/A♭
Dm7
G+5/G
For the crown of thorns you let them place on your head I say
Choir
Thank you
39
Cmin
Dm7(♯5)/C
B♭
Thank you Lord
Choir
Thank you Lord
Thank you Lord
43
B♭7/A♭
Gsus4/D
BM7(♭5)/G
For eve - ry step you carr - ied the cross so my
Thank you
47
Cmin
C+5/G♭
F7
F7
G♭7
G7
sin - ful soul would not be lost

51
G♭6(♭5)/A♭
Lead
Thank you
Choir
Thank you
Gsus4/D
Lead
Thank you
Cmin/G
Choir
Thank you
55
Cmin
Lord
Cmin
Gmin7
Cmin
Go to Chorus (M-11) then, to V2
60
Cmin/G
Cmin
C7♯5/G♭
V2. For the
E♭6(♭5)/F
nails in your
hands for the
65
G♭6(♭5)/D
nails in your
G7
feet I say
Cmin
Thank you Lord

69
B♭M/C
B♭
B♭7/A♭
Choir
Lead
Thank you Lord Thank you Lord Thank you For the wound
72
Dm7
Baug/G
in your side and the blood that came stream-ing down
75
Cmin
B♭/C
Cm/F
B♭
Cmin/E♭
Choir
I say Thank you Lord Thank you Lord Thank you Lord
79
B♭/A♭
Gsus4/D
BM7(♭5)/G
For lay - ing down your life and pick-ing it up a - gain
Thank you

83
Cmin
C+5/G♭
F7
F7
G♭7
G7
For your ho - ly spi - rit you let me feel eve - ry now and then
87
VAMP
G♭6(♭5)/A♭
Thank you
Choir
Thank You
Gsus4/D
Lead
Thank you
BM7(♭5)/G
Choir
Thank You
91
Cmin
Lead
Thank you
EM7(+5)/G♭
Choir
Thank You
E♭6(♭5)/F
Lead
Thank You Lord
G♭7
G7
Repeat as desired
Thank You Lord
95
G♭6(♭5)/A♭
Lead
Thank you
Choir
Thank you
Gsus4/D
Lead
Thank you
BM7(♭5)/G
Choir
Thank you
Cmin
Lord
Fine

THIS IS THE DAY
(Celebrate)

10
D♭ G♭ A♭/C D♭
This is the day
Re - joice Re - joice
12
D♭/F G♭ A♭ D♭
That the Lord hath made
This is the day the Lord hath made
14
D♭ G♭ A♭/C D♭ D♭/F A♭
Be glad
Re - joice Re - joice Be glad
16
Fmin7D♭ D°7 E♭min D♭/F A♭ Fmin7D♭
Be glad
in it Be glad in it

19
D°7
E♭min
Options: Repeat Verse or
Go to VAMP (M-31)
G♭/B♭
D♭sus/A♭
D♭
1.
Repeat 1 time
Re - joice
This is the day
Sopr
Re - joice
Re - joice
Re - joice
in it
22
D♭sus/A♭
D♭sus/G♭
D♭/F
2.
D♭/G♭
D♭sus/A♭
D♭/F
Verse
A - no - ther day to praise him
25
D♭/G♭
D♭sus/A♭
A♭/B♭
D♭/G♭
A - no - ther day to tell the world
Great is the Lord
28
G♭
D♭
D♭/A♭
A♭/B♭
Fmin7
D♭sus/A♭
Go to: CHORUS
and great - ly to be praised
This is the day

31 CHORUS II
D♭/F G♭ A♭ D♭ D♭ G♭
That the Lord hath made
This is the day the Lord hath made Re - joice
34
A♭/C D♭ D♭/F G♭ A♭ D♭
This is the day
That the Lord hath made
Re - joice
This is the day the Lord hath made
37
D♭ G♭ A♭/C D♭ D♭/F A♭ Fmin7D♭
Be glad
Re - joice Re - joice Be glad in it
40
D°7 E♭min D♭/F A♭ Fmin7D♭ D°7 E♭min
Be glad Re - joice
Be glad in it Re - joice

43
G♭/B♭
D♭sus/A♭
D♭
Ce - le - brate
Re - joice Re - joice in it
45
VAMP
D♭/F
G♭
Ce - le - brate
D♭/F
G♭
This is the
Ce - le - brate
Ce - le - brate
48
A♭/C
D♭
day
Ce - le - brate
D♭/F
G♭
This is the day
Ce - le - brate
50
D♭/F
G♭
A♭/C
D♭
3.
Repeat as desired
Ce - le - brate
This is the
day
Ce - le - brate
Ce - le - brate
This is the day

53
4.
A♭/C D♭ D♭/F A♭ Fmin7 D♭
day Be glad
This is the day Be glad in it
55
D°7 E♭min D♭/F A♭ Fmin7 D♭ D°7 E♭min
Be glad
Re - joice
Sopr
Be glad in it Re - joice
58
G♭/B♭ D♭sus/A♭ D♭sus/A♭ D♭
This is the day
Altos/Tenors
Re - joice Re - joice in it
60
D♭/F G♭ A♭ D♭
Fine
This is the day
This is the day This is the day

ON THE OTHER SIDE OF THROUGH

12
D♭
G♭ A♭
D♭
Fm7(♯5)/F
D♭
trod - ding through lifes mur - ky wa - ters tri - als
15
G♭
A♭
D♭
G♭
A♭
form the tears in your eyes
17
Fm7(♯5)/D♭
A♭/F
D♭
A♭/F D♭
Don't stop I'm tell - ing you
20
E♭dim/E♭
D♭/F
E♭dim/G♭
D♭/F
E♭dim/G♭
D♭/A♭
there's a bless - ing on the

Go to Verse 2 (see pg 7)
22
B♭m7(♯5)/A♭
A♭
1.
A♭
G♭
G♭/B♭
A♭/C
ot - her side of through
25
2. D♭
D°7/B♭
26
CHORUS
Fsus7♯5/E♭
A♭
D♭/A♭ E♭m
D♭/D♭
(Leader Ad-libs)
On the ot - her
28
G♭/D♭
A♭
D♭
B°7
E♭min7
A♭/B♭
G♭/A♭
D♭/B♭ E♭m/A♭
side of through there's a
31
D♭
D♭/B♭
Fsus7♯5/E♭
Fmin7
Gdim
A♭
A♭/G♭
D♭/G♭
bless - ing wai - ting for you Hold

35
Db/F
Ab/Eb
Db/A
Db/Bb
Ebm
Ddim
Ebdim
fast Hold fast your trou - bles will not last
38
Db/Gb
Ebm/Gb
Db/Ab
Db/F
Ab
There's a bless - ing Yes! a
41
Bbmin
Bbmin
Ab
Bbm/Gb
Cdim/Bb
Db/Eb
Db/Eb
bless - ing On the ot - her
44
Gb/Ab
Db
Db
Go to Verse 3 (Lyrics on pg 6)
(After VAMP to go M-57)
3.
Gb/Bb
Ab/C
side of through

Go to Chorus M-26 then, to VAMP
47
4. D♭
D°7/B♭
48
VAMP
D♭/A♭
A♭/G♭
fast
50
B♭7(♯9)
B♭7/D
E♭m
D♭/F
D♭/G♭
Hold
D♭
fast
53
A♭7/G♭
A♭/D♭
B♭
D♭/D
E♭m
55
Repeat 1x or as desired
5.
D♭/F
D♭/G♭
Hold
Go to Chorus M-35 then to 57
56
6.
D♭/F
D♭/G♭
57
D♭
Hold
through

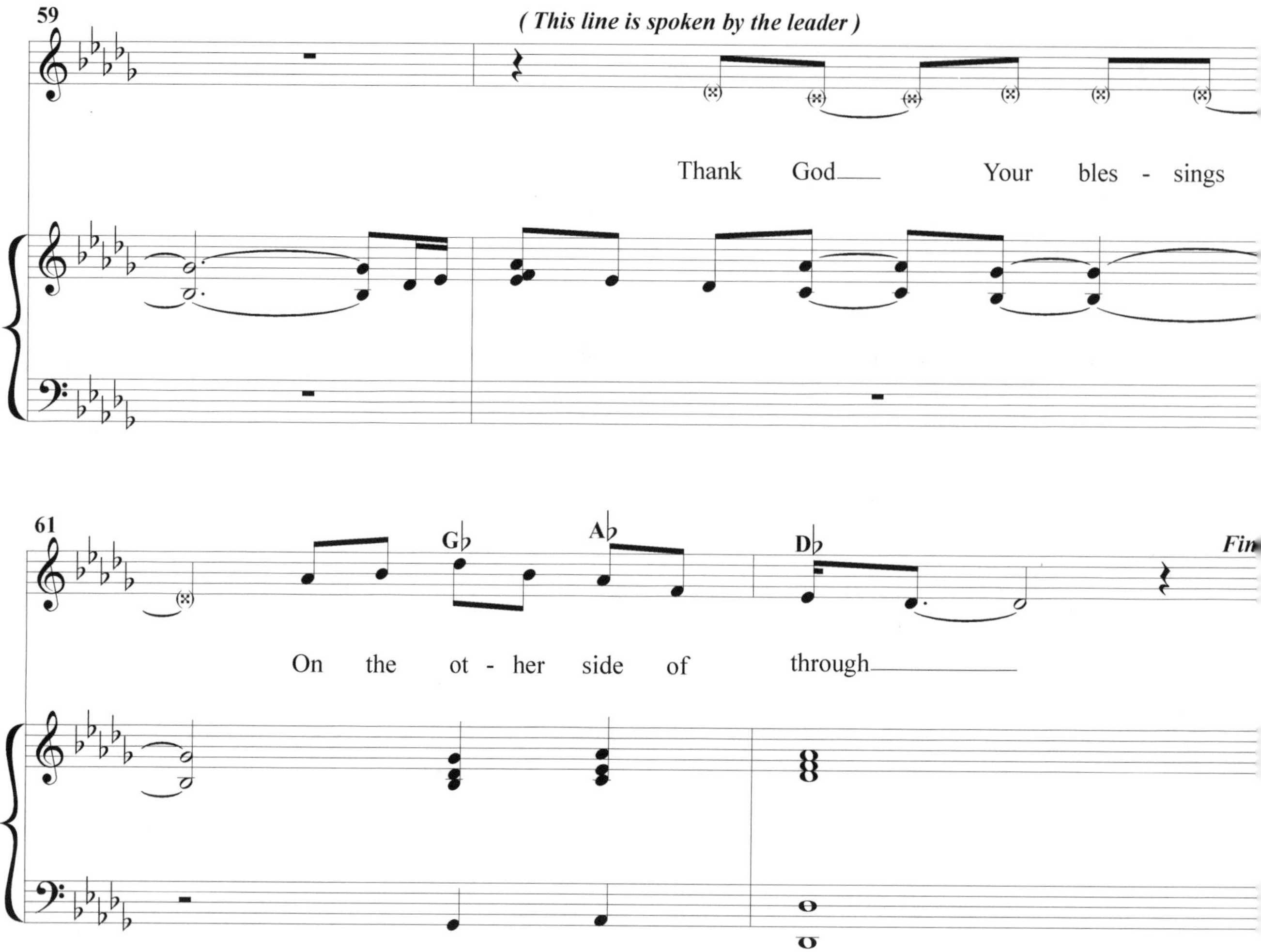

Consuslt your recording for the vocal patterns of V2, V3 & Vamp: Leader Ad-Libs

V2. We may not see the other side - the light from darkness may seem to hide
but don't give up whatever you do - the presence of God is right there with you
Don't stop, this word is for you - There's a blessing on the other side of through

V3. What God has prepared for you - is better than what you're going through
so run this race with determination - God has prepared your destination
Don't give up I'm telling you - There's a blessing on the other side of through

VAMP: Leader Ad-libs

Weeping may endure for a night - but joy will come in the morning light
Hold your head up - stick your chest out - hang on in there (hang on in there)
Hold fast in the good times - Hold in the bad,
Hold on when you're happy - and Hold on when you're sad
Hold and remember that in Jesus name - your faithfulness will not be in vain

I Came To Lift Him Up

Scored by
James Bignon

Writer / Arranger
James Bignon

11
A♭m
the Joy
up the Joy of my sal -
13
B♭m7♯5 A♭ B♭m7♯5 A♭m B♭m7♯5
I came
va - tion I came to lift him
15
A♭m B♭m7♯5 A♭ B♭min7
the Ru - ler Will you
up the Ru - ler of all na - tions
18
A♭ B♭m7♯5 A♭/C D♭ A♭/D♭ B♭m/D♭ A♭/C
Tell me will you
Will you help me will you help me

21
G♭
D♭
D♭/F
A♭
Some bo - dy help me lift him up
Some bo - dy help me lift him up
24
After Verse the 2d x, go to Bridge
3.
(Repeat Chorus: M-10, 1x then, to Verse)
I came
26
G♭/A♭
D♭/A♭
A♭
A♭ B♭m A♭
VERSE
He's the cre - a - tor of the world all pow-er is in his hands
Give him glo - ry
30
G♭/A♭
D♭/A♭
A♭
he can bring a - bout a change that no man un - der - stands

33
A♭
D♭7
D♭7
C7(♭5)
Lead
{ Unison S/A }
Let me tell you what, what he did for
Give him glo - ry
36
C7(♭5)
AM7(♭5)
C7(♭5)
AM7(♭5)
A♭m/E♭
D♭2/E♭
F7
S/A/T
me He loosed my shack - les and he set me free
39
Go to CHORUS (M-10) then, to Verse a 2nd time
G♭/A♭
BRIDGE
I came I came to lift him
I came to
I
42
D♭/A♭
A♭
G♭
D♭
A♭/E♭
G♭
I came
lift him I came to lift him up I

45
Repeat 3x's or as desired
D♭ A♭ G♭ D♭
to lift him He's
came to lift him I came to lift him
48
A♭/E♭ A♭m B♭m A♭m A♭m G♭
been so good to me I came to lift him
up been so good to me I
51
D♭ D♭/F
Repeat 1x or as desired
A♭ A♭ B♭m A♭
He's been so good He's
came to lift him up been so good to me
54
Repeat 3x's
A♭ G♭
been so good I came to lift him
been so good to me I

57
D♭
D♭/F
A♭
B♭min7
59
A♭/B♭
B♭m
A♭/C
Will you
Tell
came to lift Him
up
Will you help me
60
D♭
4.
Repeat 3 x's or as desired
me will you
Will you
will you help me
63
A♭/D♭
A♭/C
G♭
Some bo - dy
Will you help me
Some
65
D♭
D♭/F
A♭
Fine
help me lift him up
bo - dy help me lift him up

Lord, I Thank You

12
(Leader Ad-Lib)
eve - ry - thing you've done for me
14
I thank you Lord for
16
giv - ing me the vic - to - ry
18
I thank you Lord you

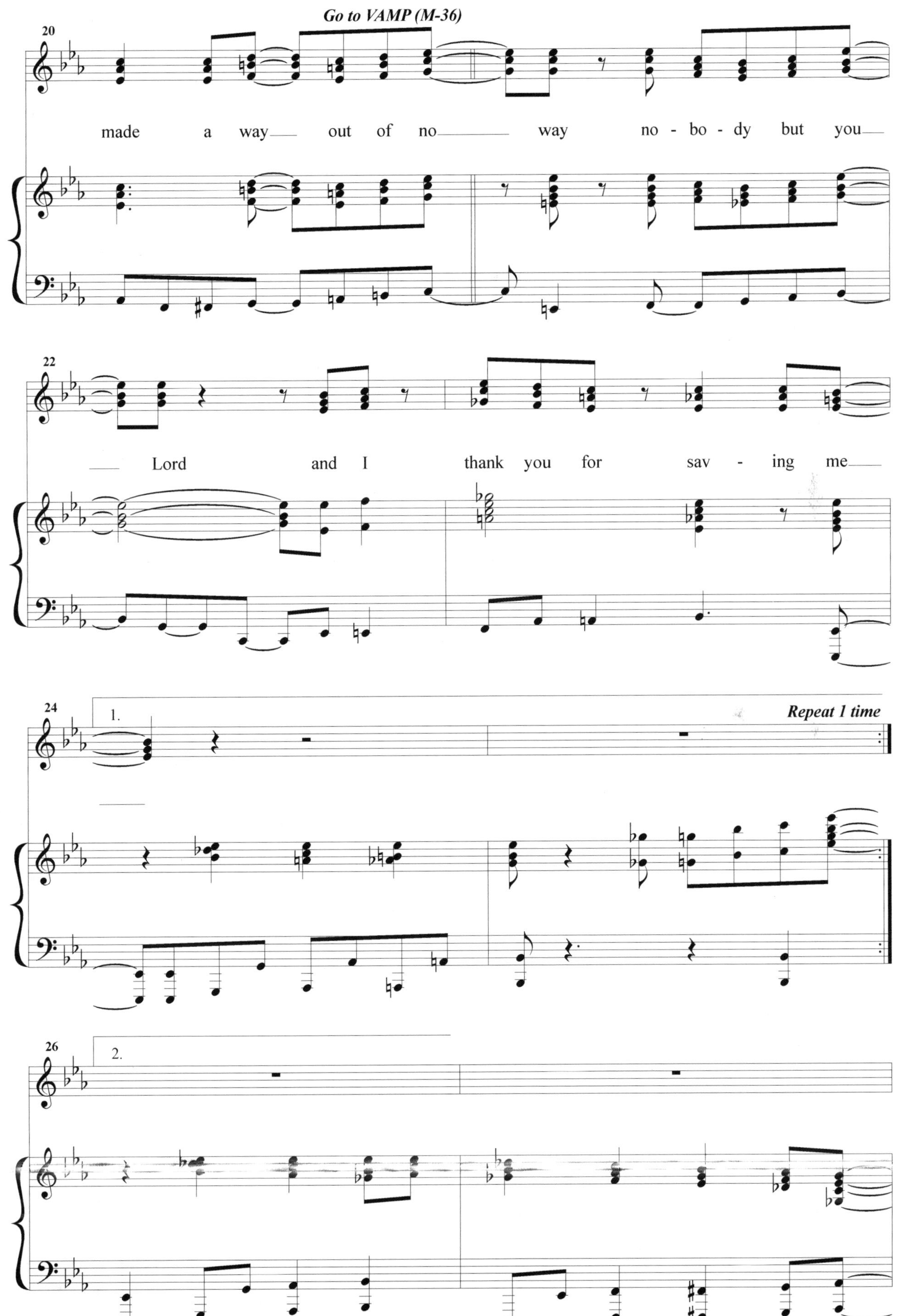
Go to VAMP (M-36)
20
made a way out of no way no - bo - dy but you
22
Lord and I thank you for sav - ing me
24
1.
Repeat 1 time
26
2.

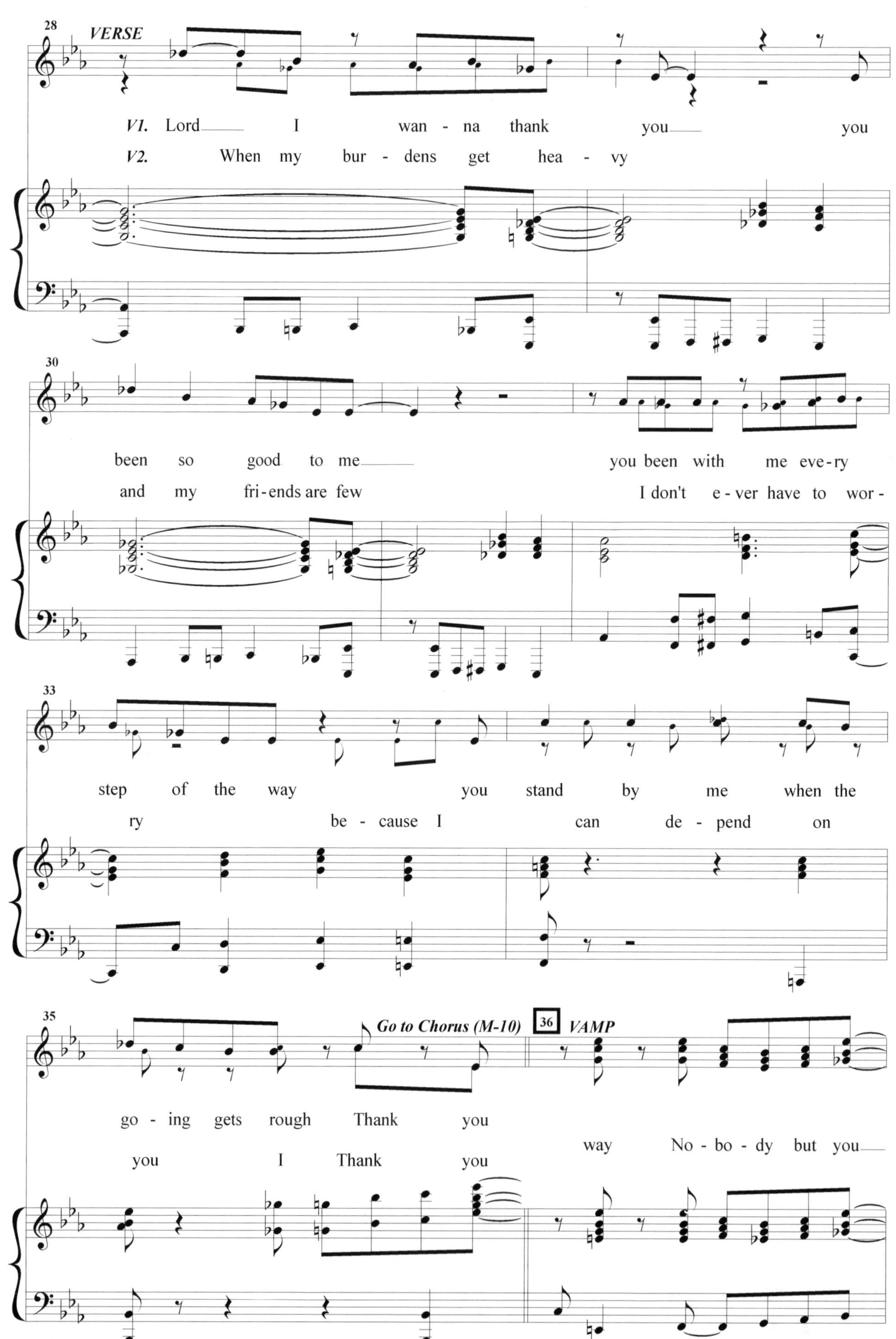

28
VERSE
V1. Lord I wan - na thank you you
V2. When my bur - dens get hea - vy
30
been so good to me you been with me eve - ry
and my fri - ends are few I don't e - ver have to wor -
33
step of the way you stand by me when the
ry be - cause I can de - pend on
35
Go to Chorus (M-10)
36
VAMP
go - ing gets rough Thank you
you I Thank you
way No - bo - dy but you

37
Lord
No - bo - dy but you Lord
Repeat 1x or as desired
40
3.
No - bo - dy but you
Lord I thank
42
you
No - bo - dy but you
44
Repeat 1x or as desired
Lord
Lord I thank

46
you Lord I thank you Lord I thank
48
4.
Repeat 1x or as desired
you Lord I thank you Lord I thank
50
you No - bo - dy but you Lord and I
52
Fine
thank you for sav - ing me

I'M GONNA DO YOUR WILL

Scored by
James Bignon

Writer / Arranger
James Bignon

11
Not know - ing what to do
Not know - ing what to do
14
I need a Sav - iour
I'm liv - ing in dark - ness
I need a
and it is
17
strong de - li - ver - er
to help me
time to find the light
here I am Lord
I'm

20
CHORUS
some - one to see me through
rea - dy to make things right
All of my
22
life
I'll
say,
Yes! Lord
25
DUET
LEAD
To eve - ry - thing you say
Lord I'll

28
fol - low all the way
CHOIR
All of my
30
*** Lead: Ad-Lib ***
life
I'll
say,
Yes! Lord
33
Go to Coda
I've
made up my mind

35
Go to Ending 2
I'm gon - na do your will
37
Go to V1
40
2.
All of my

42
*** Lead: Ad - Lib ***
Repeat as desired
made up my mind
I've
46
LEAD
I'm gon - na do your will
made up my mind
48
Fine
LEAD
your will

PRAISE THE MATCHLESS LAMB OF GOD

10
C/G
C/E♭ G/E Amin/G G/B
Asus4
Dmin C/E Dmin/F
The Lamb of God Praise the
to The Lamb of God Praise the
12
C/G
G G7/B
After V1, Go to V2 (M-23)
C C/E F C/G Dmin/G
1.
Repeat Chorus 1 time
match - less lamb of God Praise him
match - less lamb of God
14
C
G/C
V1. Wor - ship the Lord
God
16
F G C Emin7
Amin
Amin/C G/D♭
in ho - li - ness Fear the Lord

18
D7
Amin
G
C/F
C/E
Emin7
fear him all the earth
Mag - ni - fy him let your
20
F
E7
Amin
Dmin
C/G
G/B
voice be raised He is
great - ly to be
He's great - ly to be
22
Go to Chorus I (M-4)
23
C
F/A
G
C
G
A♭
A♭/C
D♭
A♭/D♭
Lead
praised Praise him
V2. Lift up your heads
praised
25
G♭
A♭
D♭
Fmin7
B♭min
B♭min/D♭
A♭/D
O! ye gates
and let the king of glo -

27
E♭7
B♭min
A♭
D♭/G♭
D♭/F
Fmin7
ry come in
Who is the king the king
29
G♭
F7
B♭min
E♭min
D♭/A♭
A♭
of glo - ry?
Je - sus is his
Je - sus is his
31
D♭
D♭/F
G♭
D♭/A♭
G♭/A♭
Chorus II
D♭
A♭
name Praise him
The King
name
Praise him The
33
G♭
A♭
D♭
F7
B♭min
A♭/D
Praise him
The Lord
King of Kings
Praise him The

35
E♭7 B♭min/E♭A♭ D♭/G♭ D♭/F D♭/E♭ D♭/F
He's wor - thy sing it from
Lord of Lords He's wor - thy sing it
37
G♭ A dim B♭min E♭min D♭/F E♭m/G♭ D♭/A♭ D♭/E Fmin7 B♭min7/A♭ A♭/C
the heart The lamb of God
from the heart Praises to the lamb of
39
B♭ D♭/D E♭min E♭m/G♭ D♭/A♭ A♭ B♭min7 A♭7/C
Praise the match - less lamb of God
God Praise the match - less lamb of
41
VAMP
D♭ D♭/F G♭ D♭/F E♭7
He's Won - der - ful Mar - ve - lous He's Glo - ri - ous
God He's Won - der - ful Mar - ve - lous

44
A♭
He's Vic - to - ri - ous
D♭
He's Wor - thy
D♭/F
Glo - ri - ous Vic - to - ri - ous He's
46
D♭
Sing it from
D♭/E♭ D♭
G♭ F7 B♭min E♭min D♭/F E♭m/G♭
Wor - thy Sing it from the heart Praises
48
D♭/A♭
The lamb of
B♭min7/A♭
Fmin7 Cdim
B♭
God Praise the
E♭min D♭/F E♭m/G♭
to the lamb of God Praise the
50
D♭/A♭
match - less lamb of God
A♭ A♭7
Repeat VAMP (M-42) 1 time or as desired
2. D♭ D♭/F D♭
D♭
Fine
God
match - less lamb of God He's God

What A Time

Scored by
James Bignon

Writer / Arranger
James Bignon

7
E♭/G
Fm/A♭
B♭m(add2)/D♭
Caug7
Fmin
TENORS
When we all get to hea - ven what a time
9
Fmin
E♭
Fmin
Fm/A♭
Fmin
E♭
Fmin
CHOIR
What a time
What a time
11
E♭/G
Fm/A♭
B♭m(add2)/D♭
Caug7
Fmin
CHOIR-UNISON
When we all get to hea - ven what a time

13
A♭7
A7
B♭7
CHOIR
B♭m(add2)/D♭
When we all
14
Caug7
Fmin
1.
D.S.
get to hea - ven what a time
What a time
16
2.
BRIDGE
17
Fmin
Cmin7
Fmin7/E♭
Gm7(♯5)/F
An - gels will be sing -

18
Fmin
E♭/G
Fm/A♭A9
B♭9
E♭
Fmin/A
ing
Joy
bells
will
be
ring -
20
Fm/B♭
Fmin
Cmin7
Fmin7/E♭
Gm7(♯5)/F
ing
There
will
be
no
more
cry -
22
Fmin
Fm/A
Fm/B♭
E♭
Fmin
Go to Coda
ing
No...
There
will
be
no
more
dy -

24
Fm/B♭
B♭m(add2)/D♭
Caug7
Fmin
CHOIR-UNISON
ing
When we all get to hea - ven what a time
26
A♭7 A7 B♭7
B♭m(add2)/D♭
Fmin
E♭/G
Caug7
Fmin
When we all get to hea - ven what a time
28
Repeat from M-17
Coda
B♭9
Fm/A♭
B♭m(add2)/D♭
An
ing
When we all

30
Caug7
Fmin
B♭m(add2)
D♭
Repeat 1x
get to hea - ven what a time
When we all
32
Caug7
Fmin
A♭7
A7
B♭7
B♭m(add2)
D♭
CHOIR
get to hea - ven what a time
When we all
34
Caug7
Fmin
Fine
get to hea - ven What a time

Magnify The Lord

CHORUS
12
S/A/T
G♭/A♭
D♭/A♭
G♭/A♭
Mag - ni - fy the lord let us ex -
14
D♭/A♭ B♭m/A♭
A♭
B♭m/A♭
A♭
G♭/A♭
D♭/A♭
alt his name to - ge - ther Mag - ni - fy the
17
Cmin7
A♭/D♭
Fmin
Cmin7
B♭min7
E♭
A♭
lord he has done great things

19
CHORUS II
G♭/A♭
D♭/A♭
Mag - ni - fy the
21
G♭/A♭
D♭/A♭
B♭m/A♭
lord let us ex - alt his name to -
23
G♭/A♭
D♭/A♭
ge - ther
Mag - ni - fy the

25
Cmin7
A♭/D♭
Fmin
Cmin7
B♭min7
E♭
A♭
lord
he
has
done
great
things
27
VAMP
G♭
Hal - le - lu - jah
29
D♭/F
G♭
Hal - le - lu - jah

31
D♭/F
A♭/E♭
Hal - le-lu - jah
G♭
34
G♭
D♭/F
A♭/E♭
D♭
Give him the high - est praise
36
G♭
D♭/F
Hal - le - lu - jah

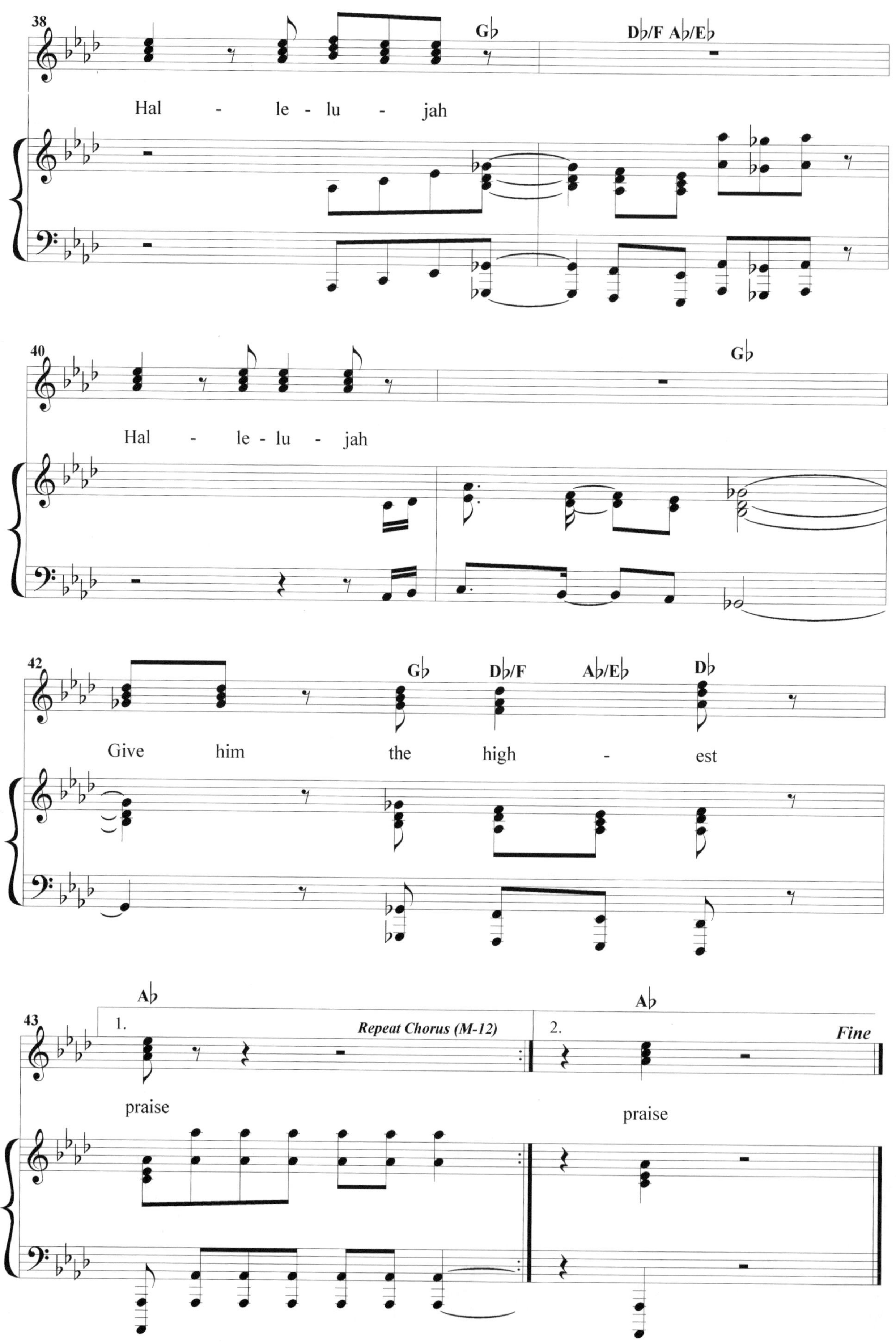
38
G♭
D♭/F A♭/E♭
Hal - le - lu - jah
40
G♭
Hal - le - lu - jah
42
G♭
D♭/F
A♭/E♭
D♭
Give him the high - est
A♭
43
1.
Repeat Chorus (M-12)
praise
A♭
2.
Fine
praise

NONE LIKE HIM

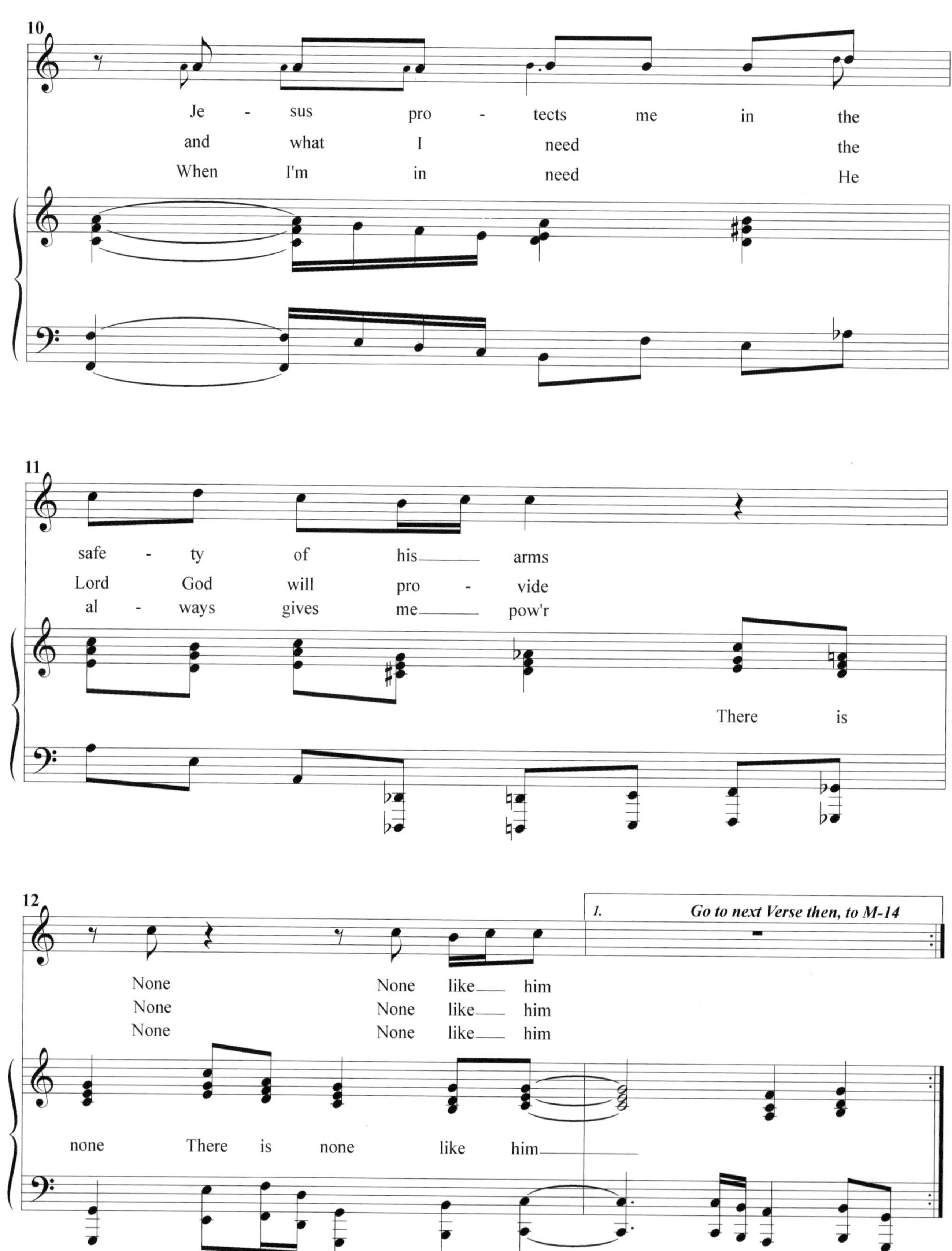
10
Je - sus pro - tects me in the
and what I need the
When I'm in need He
11
safe - ty of his arms
Lord God will pro - vide
al - ways gives me pow'r
There is
12
None None like him
None None like him
None None like him
none There is none like him
1. Go to next Verse then, to M-14

14
CHORUS II (Leader Ad-Lib)
None like him
16
None like him
No
17
None like him there is
None like him
Repeat 1x or as desired
19
VERSE
4. On Je - sus You can de - pend
If you're sick you can't find a cure

21
When friends move out The
I know a man Who'll

22
Lord will step right in None None like him
al - ways be right there None None like him
There is none There is none like him

24
2. Go to Next Verse then, to M-25

CHORUS III (Leader Ad-Lib)
None like him
None like him No
None like him there is
None like him
Repeat 1x or as desired
VERSE
6. No bet - ter friend can be found.
If you're un - ea - sy can't see your way through
If your life's un - hap - py he'll
turn it o - ver to Je - sus He

33
turn it all a round
knows just what to do
None None like him
None None like him
There is none There is none like him
35
3. & 4.
Go to Verse 7
CHORUS IV (Leader Ad-lib)
None like him
37
None like him No
None like him there is
39
5.
Repeat 1x or as desired
Fine
None like him
None like him

Heaven Belongs To You

Scored by
James Bignon

Writer / Arranger
James Bignon

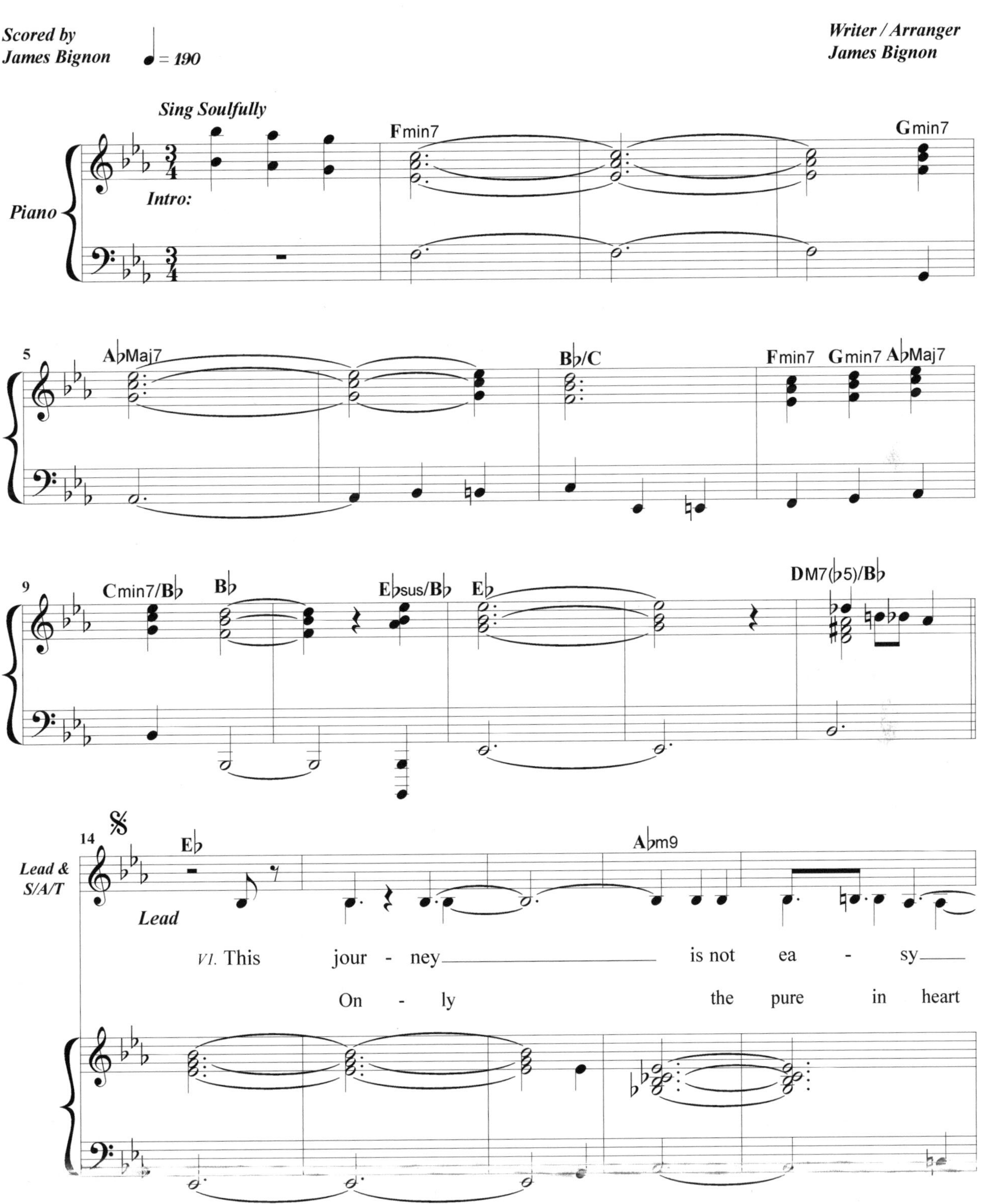

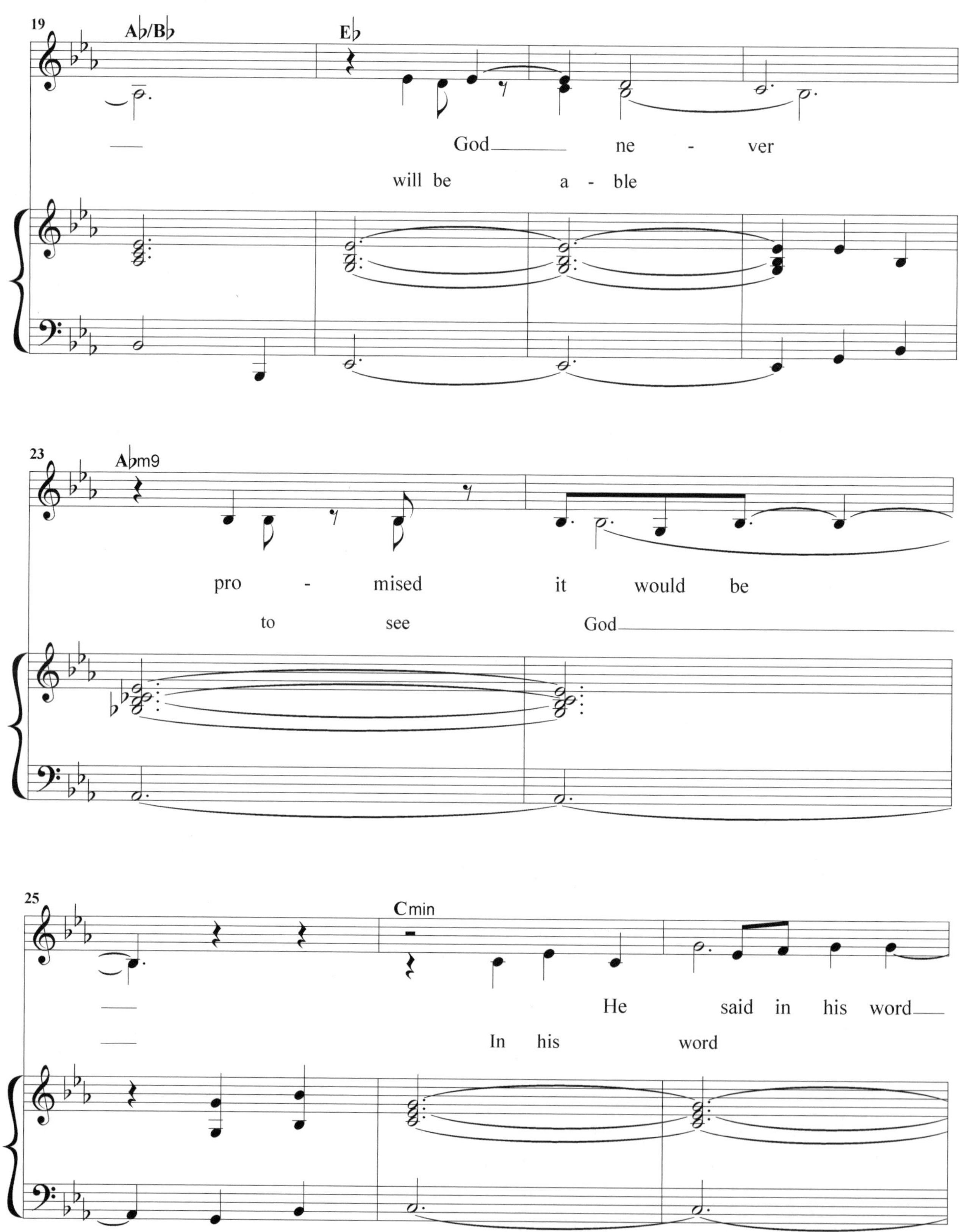
19
Ab/Bb
Eb
God ne - ver
will be a - ble
23
Abm9
pro - mised it would be
to see God
25
Cmin
He said in his word
In his word

28
Gmin7
E♭/A♭
you've
got
to
live
you must
a
-
bide
31
Cmin
ho
-
ly
if
you
wan
-
na
be
with
In
or
-
der
to
one
34
D♭9
him
for
e
-
day
be
by

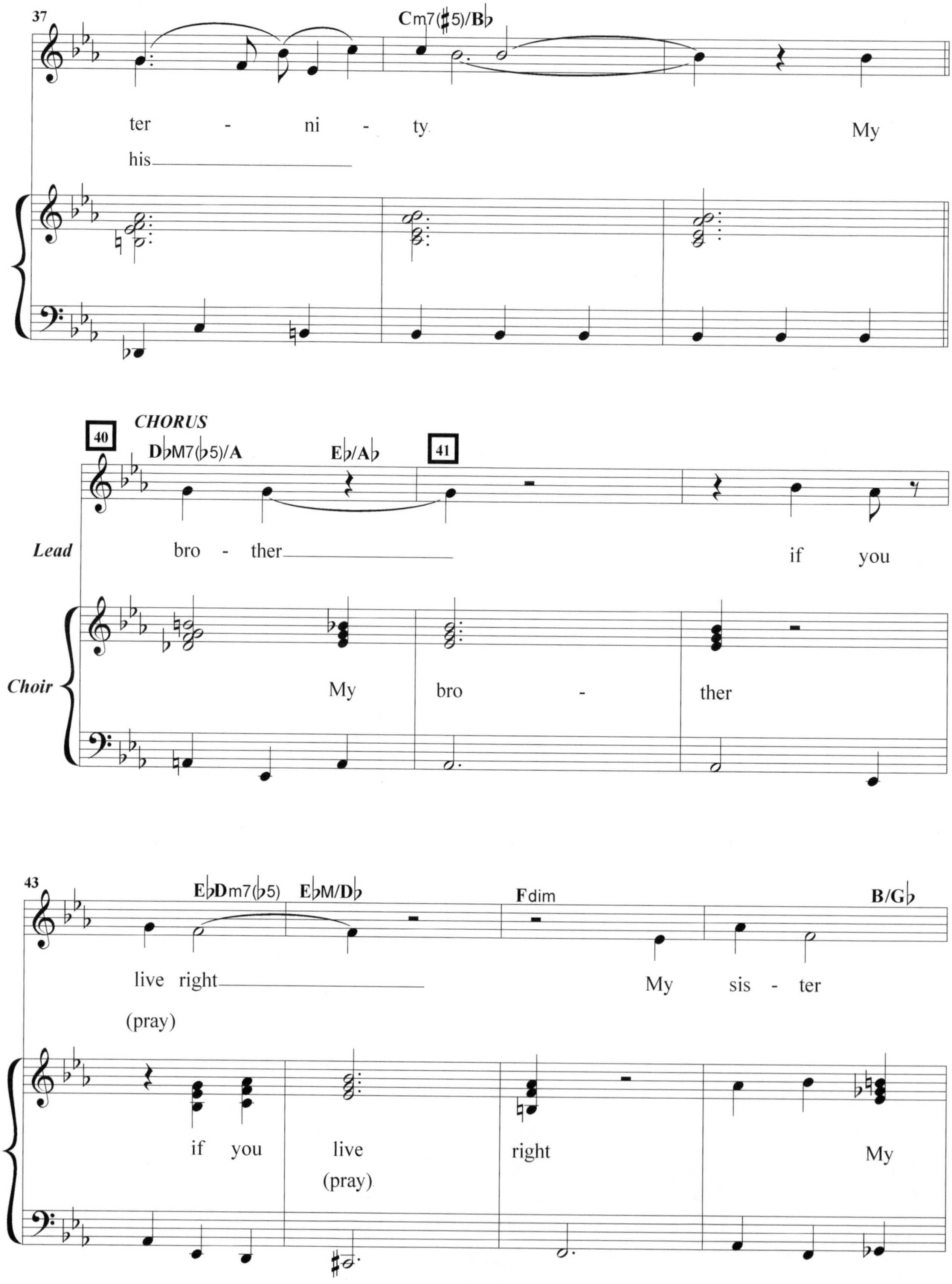

37

Cm7(♯5)/B♭

ter - ni - ty My

his

CHORUS

40

D♭M7(♭5)/A E♭/A♭

41

Lead

bro - ther if you

Choir

My bro - ther

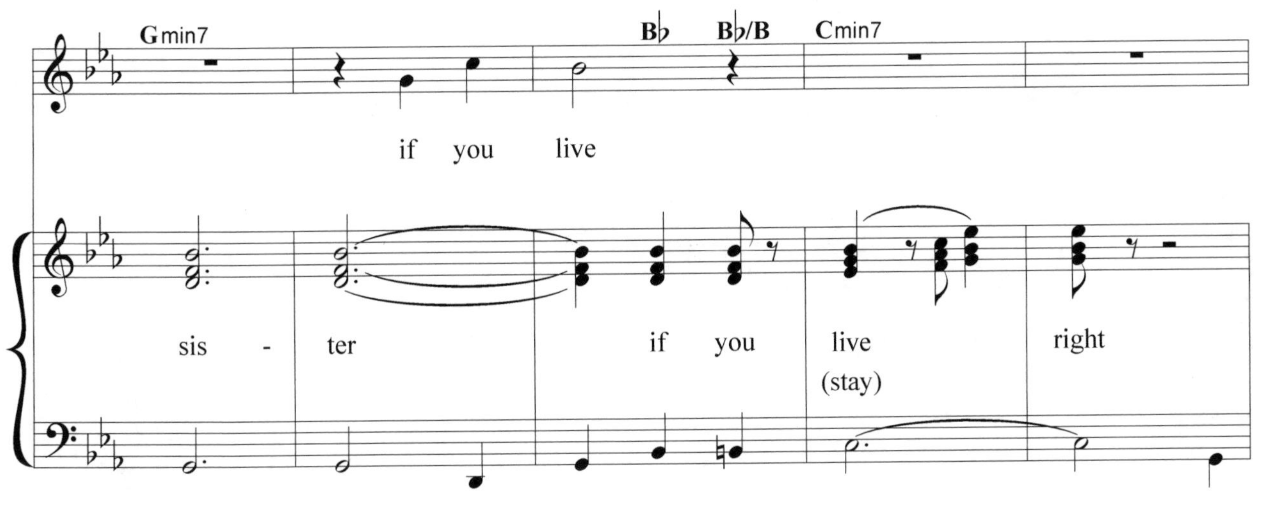
Gmin7
B♭
B♭/B
Cmin7
if you live
sis - ter
if you live
right
(stay)

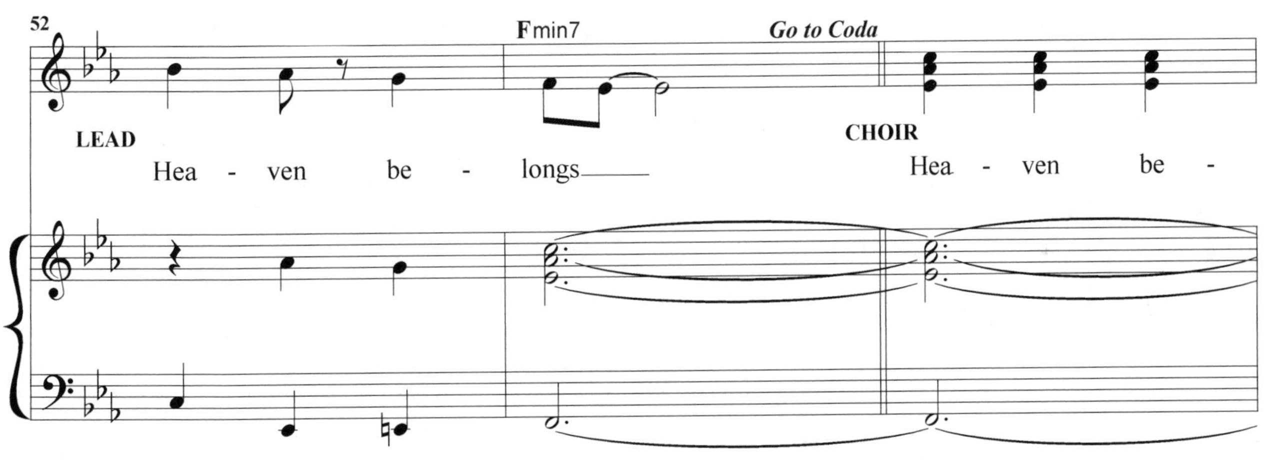
52
Fmin7
Go to Coda
LEAD
Hea - ven be - longs
CHOIR
Hea - ven be -

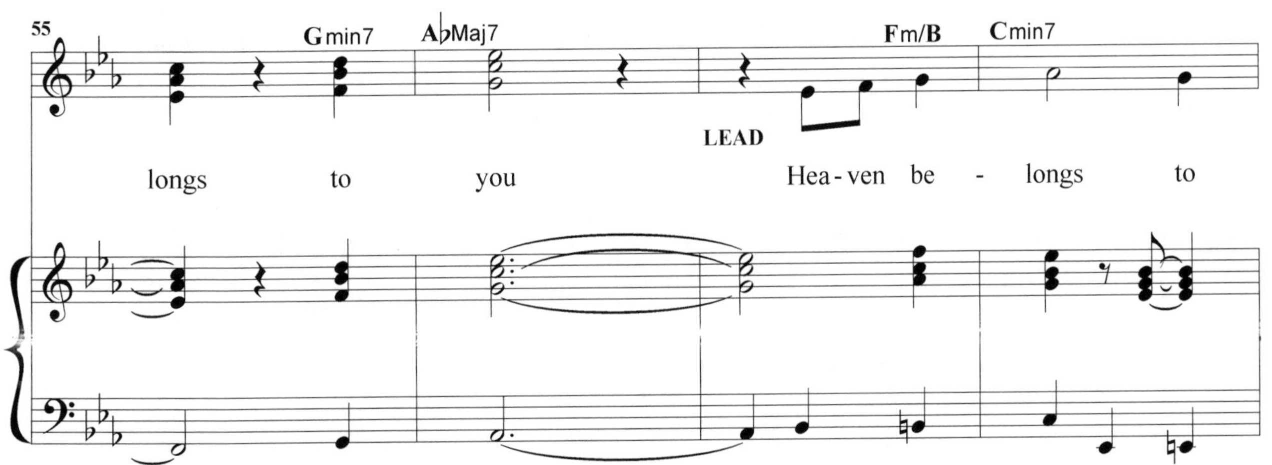
55
Gmin7
A♭Maj7
Fm/B
Cmin7
longs to you
LEAD
Hea-ven be - longs to

59
Fmin7
Gmin7
A♭Maj7
Cmin7/B♭
B♭
E♭sus4/B♭
you
Hea - ven be - longs to
1 E♭
Go to V2 (M-14)
you
65
2. E♭
E♭9sus4/B♭
Gaug7
E♭
Repeat from M-41 Line 2, to Coda
LEAD
My bro - ther
you
My

68
Fmin7
Coda
Gmin7
A♭Maj7
Hea - ven be - longs to you
71
E♭/B
B♭/C
Go to M-74
Fmin7
3, 4
[Leader Ad-lib]
LEAD
Hea - ven
74
Fmin7 Gmin7 A♭Maj7
Cmin7/B♭ B♭/G
E♭sus4/B♭
E♭
Fine
CHOIR
Hea - ven be - longs to you

Songs Written & Arranged by James Bignon
Recorded with The Deliverance Mass Choir

THE MASTERPEACE

If I Hold Out (My Change Will Come)
For The Rest of My Life
Who He Is
He Is God
More of You
Miracle

GOD IS GREAT

God Is Great
Bless His Holy Name
More Than I Can Say
To Worship Him
Glory To His Holy Name
My Offering
Praise The Name of Jesus
Thank You For Everything
Put Everything In God's Hands (Rearranged)
How Excellent Is Thy Name

MIRACLE

He Made The Difference
Miracle
Stand Up And Be Counted
I Can't Thank Him Enough
Trust In The Lord
This Is The Day
Just Because He Is Who He Is
Just For Me
God Said It Will Be Alright

ON THE OTHER SIDE OF THROUGH

Won't It Be Grand
Your Deliverance Will Come
I'm Determined
Everywhere You Go
Standing On The Promises (Rearranged)
No One Understands Like Jesus (Rearranged)

WHAT A MIGHTY GOD WE SERVE

I Came To Lift Him Up
Lord, I Thank You
Praise The Matchless Lamb of God
What A Time
Come To Jesus
I'm Gonna Do Your Will
What A Mighty God We Serve
Just Like Jesus